I believe

A Student Devotional Journal

CONCORDIA PUBLISHING HOUSE · SAINT LOUIS

Copyright © 2010 Concordia Publishing House
3558 S. Jefferson Ave., St. Louis, MO 63118-3968
1-800-325-3040 • www.cph.org

1 2 3 4 5 6 7 8 9 10   19 18 17 16 15 14 13 12 11 10

Contents

Introduction

"I believe ..."

If you grew up in a Christian church, you may recall hearing the words *I believe* on a regular basis. These two simple words form the active opening to the familiar Apostles' Creed:

> I believe in God, the Father Almighty, Maker of heaven and earth.
>
> And in Jesus Christ, His only Son, our Lord, who was conceived by the Holy Spirit, born of the Virgin Mary, suffered under Pontius Pilate, was crucified, died, and was buried. He descended into hell. The third day He rose again from the dead. He ascended into heaven and sits at the right hand of God, the Father Almighty. From thence He will come to judge the living and the dead.
>
> I believe in the Holy Spirit, the holy Christian church, the communion of saints, the forgiveness of sins, the resurrection of the body, and the life everlasting. Amen.

Perhaps you are new to the Christian faith, or you aren't quite sure about faith. In that case, these words, so well known to others, may seem foreign to you.

Regardless of your background, we all have things we understand to be true. I believe in gravity—I know that when I get up each morning, my feet will stick to the floor rather than the ceiling. I believe the sun only comes up in the east, never the west. The world we live in has certain constants; scientists like to call them *laws*. Whatever you call them, these are the constants that affect our lives.

Faith works the same way. Our faith in God and His saving work through Jesus Christ affects how we live out our lives. Through His death and resurrection, Jesus paid the price for sin, making salvation ours.

> We could never grasp the knowledge of the Father's grace and favor except through the Lord Christ. Jesus is a mirror of the fatherly heart, outside of whom we see nothing but an angry and

terrible Judge. But we couldn't know anything about Christ either, unless it had been revealed by the Holy Spirit. (Large Catechism, Part II, paragraph 65)

In this book, you'll read the faith stories of many different people. Each of their stories is unique. Some wrestled with faith questions for years; others have always known the comfort of faith in Christ.

Using This Book

This devotional journal was designed to work a bit differently from most devotional resources. In addition to sharing the faith stories from each of our authors, we wanted to provide opportunities for you to begin writing *your* story. This allows *I Believe* to go beyond being just a bunch of words on a page to become something you interact with. As you record your thoughts, *I Believe* becomes your own story as well as the stories our authors put down in print.

Following each story, we've provided opportunities for you to reflect on the author's faith narrative using a phrase from the Apostles' Creed. Along the way, you'll find quotes from the Bible–the Word of God. You'll also see quotes from the writings of scholars who have shared their wisdom and insights with the Church throughout the years.

I'm Not Sure

Jeffrey Meinz

I attended a Lutheran grade school in Farmington, Missouri. It was decided by the pastors, principal, and elders (even the librarian, Mrs. Giessing, may have had a hand in the decision) that our entire class of seventh- and eighth-grade students would receive confirmation instruction during the school week. So, once a week, our group of twenty or so students grabbed our confirmation books and ascended a flight of stairs to the auditorium of our century-old school. There we sat quietly as we were instructed by our senior pastor. I often wondered what our teacher, Mr. G., did during that free period. I imagined him in the play yard, beating all the third graders at tetherball. Maybe he was in the cafeteria, snitching a cinnamon roll. Regardless of Mr. G.'s activity, for our group of pimple-faced pupils (except for Julie Ward, whose skin was perfect), that next hour was spent filling in the blanks, memorization, and listening to Pastor Wegener discuss things like sanctification and justification. Kathy Bishop, our future class valedictorian, loved it—every minute of it. You know the type; the pastor asked a question, and Kathy raised her hand, every time. I remember thinking to myself, *Sure, I could be the valedictorian of our class if I really wanted to be!* Then I wondered if the valedictorian got any prizes, awards, or gifts for receiving such a special honor. I couldn't think of any, so I decided it was easier to be the class clown. Later, at graduation, Kathy received a small pin and a framed certificate that read "Valedictorian." I was proud of the choice I had made earlier to be a loafer. I already had pins, and I could make a certificate with my own name on it.

However, in confirmation class, I tried pretty hard. Most of the staff at St. Paul's Lutheran School in Farmington, Missouri, believed that I would grow up to be a pastor or at least a professional church worker. I figured that if I were going to avoid a D in one class, confirmation should probably be it. I assumed that there probably weren't too many pastors or professional church workers who got Ds in school, especially in confirmation class.

I must have been particularly quiet that day in confirmation class, which was unusual. Since Pastor Wegener was accustomed to my regular participation, he wondered if everything on that day—that meaningful day—was all right.

But I was in shock. Just the night before, my best friends and I had made an amazing discovery that shook the foundations of my faith.

My best friend was Scott Williams, and he and I had been together in the same class at St. Paul's since third grade. But we had friends—non-Lutheran friends—outside of our school. Doug was a Baptist and Aaron was Methodist. And the night before, the four of us had begun putting two and two together, and we realized that what we believed was a huge scam.

Doug's parents were Baptist. Aaron's parents were Methodist. Scott's and my parents were Lutheran. That night, the four of us realized that we are only what our parents are or wanted us to be.

I quickly looked around confirmation class and concluded that every classmate of mine had Lutheran parents. They worshiped in the same church I did, often in their same "assigned" pew. We weren't here because we *believed* any of this stuff; we were here because our parents wanted us here. We were being brainwashed into being believers; none of us actually *believed*, did we? My mind, with Satan's help, went from zero to sixty in an instant:

I wonder if any of this stuff is actually true! What if these lessons are just handed down generation after generation, and no one has ever considered breaking out of the mold for fear of being looked down on by their parents?

Maybe our Baptist, Methodist, and Lutheran parents just taught us what we are to believe, like they taught us to ride a bike and tie our shoelaces!

What if Jesus and eternal life are like Velcro straps, or snaps, or buckles—only one of the many ways to fasten your shoes?

Is Doug's God the same as mine? What if Doug's parents are right and my parents are wrong? What if we're all wrong and I've never even been told about the truth yet?

What if I died tonight? Would I go to heaven?

Is there even a heaven?

I spent the class in dumbfounded silence. I was shocked. How could it have taken me this long to stumble across this truth?

Praise God that Pastor Wegener had the insight to know that something was going on in the gray matter between my ears. When class ended, I gathered up my books and stumbled into rank and file to head back to our homeroom. But Pastor Wegener stopped me. The rest of the class left, and there I stood, all alone with Pastor Wegener in the auditorium.

His question was simple: "Jeffrey, what were you thinking about in confirmation today?"

That, I assumed, would be the end of it. I was about to explain to my pastor that while he was so eloquently explaining that we were "saved by grace and not by works," I had decided that I didn't want to be a Lutheran anymore. In fact, I wasn't so sure I wanted to be a *Christian* anymore. I wanted to explore things on my own, and if I found another teaching that I *knew* was true, then I'd hop on that train. Furthermore, no one had asked me or Scott Williams if we wanted to be there. In fact, no one had asked *any* of us if we wanted to be there. It was simply part of our educational day at St. Paul's. I figured that if I was a Lutheran only because my parents were Lutheran, or if I was in confirmation only because my parents wanted me there, then I wanted out. But I knew that in principle, this kind of faith wouldn't fly with God when I met Him at the end of my life.

Imagine for a moment: While my family is on vacation to Branson, Missouri, we all die in a tragic car accident. There would be God, waiting for us at the pearly gates. Jesus would be on His right. (Or was it His left? I could never remember.) God, in that deep booming voice we hear in the movies, would ask, "Jeffrey, do you believe in Jesus as the way, the truth, the life, and the only way to heaven?"

"Well, God, it's like this: My parents believe in You, and they took me to 8 a.m. church when I was little. They dropped me off at Sunday School, and they made sure I was in confirmation class during middle school. I've currently got a 97 percent in memory work, and every time I'm scheduled to acolyte, I'm there 10 minutes early. So, to answer Your earlier question, isn't it obvious? Isn't it?"

"Jeffrey," God would ask again, "do you believe in Jesus?"

"God, I'm in confirmation! What more do You want? Oh, wait, I can answer my own question: I was baptized! Whew! I dodged a close one there, didn't I? Good thing I remembered to play the Baptism card."

"Jeffrey, do you believe in Jesus?"

"Okay, God, when is the part that You tell me to feed Your lambs? Ha! Remember that time with Peter? That was good, one of my favorite parts of the Bible."

For some reason, though, I don't think that's what Jesus had in mind when He said, "You shall love the Lord your God with all your heart and with all your soul and with all your mind and with all your strength" (Mark 12:30).

Now, let's get back to Pastor Wegener, the pastor who, I was certain, would kick me out of the Lutheran Church for thinking blasphemous thoughts during confirmation.

Again, his question was simple: "Jeffrey, what were you thinking about in confirmation class today?"

"Pastor Wegener, I don't want to be a Lutheran, or even a Christian, simply because my parents are."

Then Pastor Wegener said the three words that marked the changing point in my faith in Jesus Christ, even to this very day. Over the course of nearly two decades of sermons and Bible studies, I've heard literally hundreds of thousands of words come out of Pastor Wegener's mouth. Maybe even millions. But honestly, out of all of those words, I can only remember three, and they changed my life:

"Neither do I."

Huh? *What?* Had I just heard him right? Had my pastor just agreed with me that he didn't want me to be a Lutheran just because my parents were? Wasn't it part of his job to make as many people Lutheran as possible? As a young teenager, I assumed that it was his responsibility to make non-Lutherans Lutheran and to keep the Lutherans faithful so they would be lifelong Lutherans. The thought even crossed my mind, *Ooh, if Pastor's boss knew about what he just said, he could get fired!* Then I realized that I couldn't think of anyone that had a bigger office than Pastor, so the only person that could fire Pastor was God. Yikes! I had heard about people being struck by lightning because of something they said that made God mad. I was sure God was just charging up a big blast aimed straight at Pastor. I took a generous step backward. Sure, what I had said and was thinking was bad, but I was only in seventh or eighth grade. God didn't honestly expect that much from me. Pastor, on the other hand, was—well, a *pastor*. He couldn't say what he had just said and not pay the price. I took a second step backward and made sure I was wearing rubber-soled shoes.

"Let me get this straight," I whispered. "You don't want me to be a Lutheran just because my parents are Lutheran either?"

"Nope."

I took another step back and bumped into the wall. There was nowhere else to go. If Pastor didn't stop making God mad, I might get taken down with him.

"Jeffrey," Pastor began, "if you are Lutheran only because your parents told you to be or because you felt like you had to, what good is that? God wants your heart. God is calling you to believe. At some point in your life, you'll become a Christian because you believe in God through the power of the Holy Spirit." (I realize that earlier I said that I only remember three of Pastor Wegener's words to me over the course of my life, and this quote behaves like I remember those words too. Technically, I don't. But he said something *like* that.)

At that moment, I began wrestling with God. It wasn't wrestling like Jacob did in the Old Testament. It was much less dramatic, but it was important nonetheless. I began by talking to Doug, Aaron, their parents, my parents, Wayne (our church's volunteer youth director), and even my older sister. I knew this was serious when I asked my older sister for her opinion. I honestly had never cared about her opinion before this, but I was serious, maybe even *worried*, so I asked everyone about matters of faith, God, the Bible and church.

In a relatively short period of time, I found myself in my bedroom in our home just outside Farmington, and I prayed to God . . . *really* prayed to God. Of course, I had asked Him before to "Come, Lord Jesus, be our guest . . ." and "I pray, dear Lord, my soul to keep. . . ." But I had never prayed, *really prayed*, from the depths of my heart. For the first time, I talked to God like He really existed in my life. For the first time, I opened the Bible not because I *had* to, but because I *wanted* to. I began memorizing verses not because they were required as part of our confirmation curriculum, but because God told us to in His Word.

All of this occurred before Confirmation Sunday of my eighth-grade year. When I stood in front of the congregation at St. Paul's Lutheran Church, wearing my white gown and red carnation, I sincerely confirmed my faith, which began in my Baptism and is still growing today.

Jeffrey Meinz Jeffrey grew up in southern Missouri where his father taught him how to fish and his mother taught him how to cross-stitch. His favorite baseball team is the Los Angeles Dodgers. He is married to his beautiful wife, Amy, and they have four amazing children. His favorite hobbies are hiking and camping in his current home state, Colorado. You can find Jeffrey on Facebook. He humbly requests that you fertilize his FarmVille crops.

I believe in God . . .

If you grew up in church, you've heard these words at least a thousand times. But have you ever thought about what they really say? Consider the very first word of the Apostles' Creed—"I." Why do you suppose the Creed begins with "I" even though we usually recite these words when we are part of a larger group of people?

In "I'm Not Sure," Jeffrey struggled with what he really believed about God. Note again Pastor Wegener's surprising reply. How did this response invite further conversation?

What concepts of faith have you struggled with? To whom or to what have you looked for answers?

I believe in God . . .

In the Large Catechism, Martin Luther establishes why he thinks the Apostles' Creed is so important for the believer:

> The Creed . . . sets forth to us everything that we must expect and receive from God. To state it quite briefly, the Creed teaches us to know Him fully. (Large Catechism, Part II, paragraph 1).

What have you learned about God from the Creed?

What things would you still like to know about God?

The Creed goes beyond being simply a statement of belief; it is also a call to action. In the Large Catechism, it says:

> We could say much here, if we were to wander, about how few people believe this article. For we all pass over it, hear it, and say it. Yet we do not see or consider what the words teach us. For if we believed this teaching with the heart, we would also act according to it. (Large Catechism, Part II, paragraphs 20–21)

How does God empower us, as His forgiven and redeemed children, to live according to what the Creed teaches?

I believe in God . . .

D A Y • T H R E E

The Book of Concord contains the documents that serve as the theological framework for doctrine in the Lutheran Church. "A General Introduction to the Book of Concord" says:

> What could possibly be so important that you would stake eternity on it? What gives a person such courage and conviction? Only one thing—the truth. This is what this book is all about, the truth of God's Word.

> God's people have always spoken this way. For example, the psalmist wrote, "I will speak of Your testimonies before kings and shall not be put to shame" (Psalm 119:46). Peter confessed his faith when Jesus asked him what he believed, "You are the Christ, the Son of the living God" (Matthew 16:16). Paul wrote, "Since we have the same spirit of faith according to what has been written, 'I believed, and so I spoke,' we also believe, and so we also speak" (2 Corinthians 4:13). (*Concordia: The Lutheran Confessions*, page xiii)

We live in a world that seeks the truth but doesn't necessarily recognize the truth found in God's Word. What one truth in God's Word is especially important to you?

How would you respond to those who are looking for truth in places other than the Word of God?

I believe in God . . .

Living by faith enables believers to boldly face challenges in their world. The author of Hebrews writes about some of these bold faithful in Hebrews 11. If you have time, read all of the great "by faith" chapter.

> Now faith is the assurance of things hoped for, the conviction of things not seen. For by it the people of old received their commendation. By faith we understand that the universe was created by the word of God, so that what is seen was not made out of things that are visible. (Hebrews 11:1–3)

What faith challenges has God given you?

How has God worked in you through faith to meet these challenges?

I believe in God . . .

D A Y • F I V E

Paul's Letter to the Romans focuses on issues of faith and belief.

> But the righteousness based on faith says, "Do not say in your heart, 'Who will ascend into heaven?'" (that is, to bring Christ down) or "'Who will descend into the abyss?'" (that is, to bring Christ up from the dead). But what does it say? "The word is near you, in your mouth and in your heart" (that is, the word of faith that we proclaim); because, if you confess with your mouth that Jesus is Lord and believe in your heart that God raised Him from the dead, you will be saved. For with the heart one believes and is justified, and with the mouth one confesses and is saved. (Romans 10:6–10)

For centuries, mankind has looked for new ways to express the faith. The results include some of the most fantastic painting, sculpture, and architecture ever known. "Through His Word, God calls forth the words we speak back to Him" (Large Catechism, Part II, note on Article I). In what ways can you speak back the words God has given you?

Notes

Throwing Caution to the Wind
Bill Yonker

Love can be so bold. Love can throw caution to the wind!

When I was a ninth grader, basketball was my life. I was immersed in it. I felt at my best with a leather ball stamped with "Spalding" or "Voit" in my hands. Coach Van Haaften led us through a spellbinding, victorious season when we lost only one game. Often I experienced a heady, euphoric feeling at the end of the game when I saw the closing seconds tick away and we ended up winning. With sweat pouring down my face, my legs exhausted, and my heart thumping, I felt life coursing through my veins. I can still conjure up in my memory the thrill I felt as we delighted in conquering our valiant, vanquished opponents. It was the best—except for one game.

Our games were played in the late afternoon. Our home court was at Grand Haven (Michigan) Junior High, which housed the seventh, eighth, and ninth grades. This junior high was just a couple of baseball throws from my house. The fateful game was played at home against our archrivals from the neighboring town, the Spring Lake Lakers. The good news is that we trounced those rich boys from Spring Lake. They were supreme boaters, sailors, and skiers, but they were no match for us freshman Buccaneers. The game was never close, and so for most of the fourth quarter, Coach had us starters on the bench, cheering on the second- and third-string boys. But even with the starters out of the game, we kept building the lead over the financially advantaged, athletically disadvantaged lads of Spring Lake. From our seats on the bench, my teammates and I whooped and hollered and cheered every dribble, every shot, every play our guys made.

I didn't notice my mom climb down from the stands and walk down the side of the court. I didn't see her until she was standing right in front of me as I was sitting on the bench with the game still being played. Too shocked, I didn't move when she leaned over, cupped my face in her hands, looked me in the eye, and said, "I'm very proud of you." She then kissed my cheek and added, "I'm going home now to fix dinner. See you at home." Then, with a wave of her hand, she sauntered out of the gym.

Of course, my cheeks were blazing red as my buddies pushed and lightly punched me, making kissing noises, telling me how "sweet" it was that my "momma" had stopped by for a goodbye kiss. I was terribly embarrassed, but this gave way to anger and frustration. Didn't my mom know what the rules were? Didn't she understand that that kind of display was not acceptable?

Ah, but didn't *I* understand how bold love can be? Didn't I know that love can throw caution to the wind?

I love Jesus' story of the prodigal son in Luke 15:11-32. Mostly I love the actions of the son's father. After the boy takes his inheritance without his dad dying, he squanders it on lousy living. He ends up destitute and hungry. Coming to his senses, the boy decides to go home, hoping Dad will take him on as a hired hand. Jesus says that "while he was still a long way off" (v. 20), his father sees him coming. One gets the sense the father was looking for his son all along. Then the story says the father *runs* to the son. Later we're shown that the son represents each one of us who has wandered away or run away from God. The father is God the Father Himself. I love that part: the Father *runs*. This is the only time in Scripture we get a picture of God running. Notice, He's not running *from* us but *to* us. And then we see the spectacular. God doesn't run to punish or push away or even to scold. He runs to welcome, to accept, to forgive, to *love*. Even more noteworthy is the fact that in Jesus' day, grown, dignified men didn't show their ankles or the calves of their legs. That was considered unsightly, vulgar, and even perverse. So men wore long flowing robes. That means that the father Jesus tells us about in the story had to hike up his robes and throw caution and dignity to the winds so he could run to welcome his son! And then it says in the original language of the New Testament that the "father fell on the son's neck" and kissed him. This means that the dad tackled the boy! So great was the dad's love, so exuberant was the dad's joy, he *tackled* his son and kissed him! Jesus is aching to show us how bold God's love is for us.

And it *is* bold! It is bold enough to love us in spite of our sin. It is bold enough to have God's Son, clothed in humanity from the Virgin's womb, take our place of punishment by suffering agony, death, and hell. It is bold enough to have that very Son, Jesus, rise from the dead and ascend into heaven so we can be welcomed home to God's mansion for all eternity. Indeed, love can throw caution to the wind.

I really have to restrain myself at my kids' sporting events. See, I am of the heart and hearth of my mother, Lois Ann Yonker. Bursts of love erupt out of me at inappropriate times as they do out of her. But we're in good company. We have a heavenly Father who always bursts with love for us and is unafraid, unashamed, and unhindered in expressing His never-ending forgiveness, love, and acceptance. I wish I had understood back in ninth grade how love could be so bold. See, there are times now when I wish my mom were as mobile as she once was (her stroke keeps her close to home). Guess I would really like it if after I finished a passionately given sermon, she would walk up to the pastor's chair, lean over, cup my face in her hands, say she is proud of me, and seal it with a kiss. But I will delight in knowing that it once happened, and I will thrill to know that our heavenly Father will continually be bold and throw caution to the wind as He loves us.

Bill Yonker When he's not enjoying his family or shepherding the folks of Immanuel Lutheran Church in East Dundee, Illinois, Pastor Yonker loves to travel around the country, talking to people about Jesus. Even though he lives in Illinois, Bill was born in Milwaukee, and he is a true blue "cheesehead" devoted to Wisconsin and the Green Bay Packers. Pastor Yonker loves good comedy (Martin Lawrence); movies that make you think and sometimes cry (*Blindside*); books that make you stay up late into the night (anything by Harlan Coben, Daniel Silva, Tami Hoag and their ilk); and songs that make you want to dance ('60s bubble gum, anyone?). Because he lives in Chicagoland, he wrinkles his nose at bad pizza, ketchup on hot dogs, and football games that are not played outside. Things that are always good for him are a cup of strong coffee, a bowl of hot soup, a Beach Boys song, riding in his Dodge Charger, browsing through bookstores, afternoon naps, Dove chocolate, and flying first class. Besides spending time with his wife, Joanne, and three children, pastoring, and speaking, you can usually find Pastor Yonker reading or writing, which are his other passions. You can get in touch with Bill via e-mail at pastoryonker@hotmail.com

... the Father Almighty, maker of heaven and earth.

When was the last time you thought about the daily care your heavenly Father provides? Like the very best possible earthly father, our God cares about every aspect of our lives. Luther wrote in the Large Catechism:

> We ought, therefore, daily to recite this article. We ought to impress it upon our mind and remember it by all that meets our eyes and by all good that falls to us. Wherever we escape from disaster or danger, we ought to remember that it is God who gives and does all these things. In these escapes we sense and see His fatherly heart and His surpassing love toward us. (Large Catechism, Part II, paragraph 23)

Think about the last time you escaped disaster or danger. What was the situation? How did your heavenly Father work out your guidance and protection?

How does God use your earthly parent to provide for your needs and protection?

... the Father Almighty, maker of heaven and earth.

In his Letter to the Church at Ephesus, Paul reminds us of reasons we have to thank our heavenly Father.

> For this reason I bow my knees before the Father, from whom every family in heaven and on earth is named, that according to the riches of His glory He may grant you to be strengthened with power through His Spirit in your inner being, so that Christ may dwell in your hearts through faith—that you, being rooted and grounded in love, may have strength to comprehend with all the saints what is the breadth and length and height and depth, and to know the love of Christ that surpasses knowledge, that you may be filled with all the fullness of God.
>
> Now to Him who is able to do far more abundantly than all that we ask or think, according to the power at work within us, to Him be glory in the church and in Christ Jesus throughout all generations, forever and ever. Amen. (Ephesians 3:14–21)

List some examples of how God the Father cares for you.

How can you share God's care with others who are in need both physically and spiritually?

... the Father Almighty, maker of heaven and earth.

In the Large Catechism, Martin Luther poses a simple, childlike example of how a believer could describe our heavenly Father:

> It is as if you were to ask a little child, "My dear, what sort of a God do you have? What do you know about Him?" The child could say, "This is my God: first, the Father, who has created heaven and earth. Besides this One only, I regard nothing else as God. For there is no one else who could create heaven and earth." (Large Catechism, Part II, paragraph 11)

Think back to your younger years. What was your vision of God when you were a child? How has your impression of God changed as you have grown older?

What simple language could you use to describe God the Father to someone who does not know Him as Lord?

. . . the Father Almighty, maker of heaven and earth.

What is the greatest or most expensive gift you've ever received? Who gave you this gift?

Our heavenly Father gives us gifts greater than we can image. As Luther says,

> For here we see how the Father has given Himself to us, together with all creatures, and has most richly provided for us in this life. We see that He has overwhelmed us with unspeakable, eternal treasures by His Son and the Holy Spirit. (Large Catechism, Part I, paragraph 24)

List some of the "unspeakable, eternal treasures" God the Father gives you.

... the Father Almighty,
Maker of heaven and earth.

D A Y • F I V E

The psalmist celebrated the work of God the Father in creation.

> By the word of the LORD the heavens were made,
> and by the breath of His mouth all their host.

> He gathers the waters of the sea as a heap;
> He puts the deeps in storehouses.

> Let all the earth fear the LORD;
> let all the inhabitants of the world stand in awe of Him!
> For He spoke, and it came to be;
> He commanded, and it stood firm. (Psalm 33:6–9)

In your opinion, what's the most amazing part of God's created world? Why is this so amazing to you?

What are some ways you can celebrate the wonders of the Father's creation?

Notes

Punched for Jesus
Paul T. McCain

I got punched the day I first dared to be a Lutheran. I grew up in the Deep South, and the public high schools in my hometown were really bad. The year I was in the eighth grade at my Lutheran grade school, there was a big race riot on the campus of Escambia County High School, the very school I was assigned to go to in a few months! Seems some people at the school were not too thrilled with the name of their mascot and all sports teams, the Rebels. The raising of the "Stars and Bars" Confederate flag on the school's flagpole one day caused a race riot, complete with gunshot wounds and stabbings. My parents thought that sending me to a place where racism and rioting were team sports wasn't such a good idea. So they sent me to Pensacola Catholic High School.

One day in religion class, Father Foley, direct from Ireland, was telling us how and why the Roman Catholic Church teaches that Buddhists, Hindus, and Muslims, if they believe what they believe sincerely, will go to heaven, even if they don't know or believe in Jesus. I politely raised my hand and asked, "Father Foley, if what you are saying is true, why did God bother to send His Son, Jesus, to die on the cross for our sins?" I remember quoting the verse I learned in confirmation class, Acts 4:12: "There is salvation in no one else, for there is no other name under heaven given among men by which we must be saved." Father Foley got red in the face and tried to change the subject. He was clearly uncomfortable.

And then it happened. A guy reached over and let me have it—pow! I got punched hard for sticking up for Jesus and daring to be Lutheran. After a class, a few others felt it was important to underscore the point, so they beat me up good and proper.

That experience more than any other helped convince me that I had better really dig into the teachings of my Lutheran faith and really understand what it means to be, and remain, Lutheran. I had to go to Mass at least once a month for four years. I sat respectfully without participating, but I was listening intently. I was continually bothered by things I heard that did not square with what I had been taught in my confirmation instruction. It was a very good learning experience. I was surrounded by people—perhaps as you are—who didn't really think that what you believe matters that much, just as long as you are a kind person who is sincere. That's pretty much the view many people take today about religion.

After I graduated from Roman Catholic high school, I didn't want to have anything to do with anything that even *looked* Roman Catholic. If it looked or sounded even remotely Roman Catholic to my eyes and ears, I was angry! I hated it! I thought that if I could get as far away from Romanism as possible in outward things, I would not have to worry about falling into the errors of Rome in doctrine.

I was wrong. I learned more about the Lutheran Church and its history. I remember reading for the first time in the Augsburg Confession, our most important Lutheran Confession, how our fathers in the faith never intended to do anything contrary to the truly "catholic" or "universal" Church but to correct errors. It dawned on me that what is truly catholic is not necessarily Roman, and what is wrong with Roman doctrine is actually deeply anti-Christian and therefore not catholic at all! That was quite a revelation to me. And so now, I rejoice in the good customs and traditions of the historic Lutheran Church.

And do you want to hear something I've not told many people? (Well, at least not until now.) One big reason I'm a Lutheran pastor today is because so many of the priests and nuns and monks at my Roman Catholic high school, each in his or her own kind way, quietly urged me to become a Lutheran pastor. In both my junior and senior years in high school, they awarded me "Religion Student of the Year" honors. I worked really hard to explain and understand carefully what they believed as Roman Catholics and to understand what I believed as a Lutheran. As wrong as they were in many of their important beliefs, God used my Roman Catholic teachers to set me on a path that has led me to where I am today—and it all began the day I got beat up for speaking up for Jesus.

The whole experience was a major wake-up call for me. I could drift through life, unconcerned about the details of the Christian faith. I could simply allow myself to be lazy about things pertaining to my faith, and just shrug my shoulders and pretend that differences among Christians do not matter. I could pretend that it doesn't even matter what a person believes at all, about anything. Or I could learn as much as I could learn about my Lutheran faith and how clearly it teaches and proclaims Jesus, and I could work to share that with others. God's Holy Spirit led me to the correct choice: dare to be, and remain, Lutheran and be committed to a life of Christianity that does not settle for second-best or a "who cares" attitude. Stand for something rather than nothing—that's the lesson I learned.

I wonder what it is in your life, right now, as you read this, that is challenging you in your faith. I wonder what kinds of questions you have in your mind, raised by your teachers or your friends. I'm sure, like me, you have a lot of questions, and perhaps, like me, you have had your share of doubts. But I know, just as it happened to me, the Holy Spirit is right there for you, to strengthen you, to encourage you, and to bless you. You know what you have been taught and who has taught it to you. Perhaps you have been taught a lot; maybe not as much. But in either case, there is always more to know and to learn.

Being a follower of Jesus who dares to be Lutheran is not easy. It's a challenge. It is stepping away from the mainstream, popular views of what it means to be religious, or even what it means to be a Christian. It is taking up a cross and following Jesus. That is both a joy and a blessing.

Maybe you'll get smacked around a bit when you dare to be Lutheran. Jesus went through worse than that for you, and He'll see you through whatever might happen when you dare to be faithful to Him. No matter what it is, Christ is there, with you, by your side, with His good gifts and Spirit!

Paul T. McCain Paul McCain is a pastor and publisher, serving at Concordia Publishing House. His interests include theology, art, music, history, digital photography, and the shooting sports—oh, and coffee, good coffee. He also enjoys the St. Louis Cardinals, particularly when they win. He married his best friend nearly thirty years ago, and the Lord has blessed their marriage with three great kids: Paul, John, and Mary. Their home also includes one dog and one cat who get along great, probably because the cat is larger than the dog. You can keep up with Paul on Facebook at: http://www.facebook.com/paultmccain or Twitter: http://www.twitter.com/paultmccain. Paul also maintians a very active blog site: http://www.cyberbrethren.com.

And in Jesus Christ . . .

Think about the worst situation you've ever been in; perhaps you broke your mom's favorite vase, or it's something much, much worse. No matter how difficult your personal situation, it pales in comparison to our situation as sinners in need of a Savior. As Martin Luther put it:

> There was no counsel, help, or comfort until this only and eternal Son of God—in His immeasurable goodness—had compassion upon our misery and wretchedness. He came from heaven to help us. (Large Catechism, Part II, paragraph 29)

"Misery and wretchedness"—now *that's* a tough situation, but it's exactly the position we were in without Jesus as our Lord and Savior. Thanks be to God that He had compassion on our sinful condition and sent Jesus as the solution to sin.

As you journal today, consider the amazing message of the Gospel. How can we share the message of hope that is ours as children of God with those who are still lost in their personal misery and wretchedness?

And in Jesus Christ . . .

Critics of the Christian faith often try to point out seeming discrepancies between biblical accounts. Sometimes fellow believers are frustrated by the seeming "missing pieces" in the story of Jesus' life. (The Bible only records two events in the life of Jesus between His birth and age 30.) The apostle John addresses this concern in his Gospel:

> Now Jesus did many other signs in the presence of the disciples, which are not written in this book; but these are written so that you may believe that Jesus is the Christ, the Son of God, and that by believing you may have life in His name. . . . Now there are also many other things that Jesus did. Were every one of them to be written, I suppose that the world itself could not contain the books that would be written. (John 20:30–31, 21:25)

John speculates that if man attempted to record every incident in the life of Jesus, there wouldn't be space enough to record the details in all of the world's books. The reality is that we have all the information about Jesus we need. By the inspiration of the Holy Spirit, the Scripture writers recorded just the information we need to know. Jesus was born to a human mother, lived a perfect life, was arrested and falsely tried, died a horrible and painful death, rose from the dead, and ascended to heaven, where He prepares our eternal home. We confess these very things as we speak the words of the Apostles' Creed each week.

Reread the words of this section of the Creed as you record these events in the life of Jesus in your own words.

And in Jesus Christ . . .

The coming of the Holy Spirit empowered Jesus' disciples to boldly speak the truth concerning Jesus Christ as Lord and Savior. When Peter and John were called before the council in Jerusalem to answer charges concerning their teaching in the temple, Peter stepped forward boldly and said:

> Let it be known to all of you and to all the people of Israel that by the name of Jesus Christ of Nazareth, whom you crucified, whom God raised from the dead—by Him this man is standing before you well. This Jesus is the stone that was rejected by you, the builders, which has become the cornerstone. And there is salvation in no one else, for there is no other name under heaven given among men by which we must be saved. (Acts 4:10–12)

Think about his audience. Here are the folks who actively worked and schemed to bring about Jesus' crucifixion. Peter takes these religious leaders to task, showing them the errors in their actions. But he doesn't leave them with this message, and he points them to the cross: "Salvation is found in no one else."

Think about your experience in worship. How do we hear the same messages of Law and Gospel each week?

Whom has God put in your life to remind you of that Law-and-Gospel balance?

And in Jesus Christ . . .

D   A   Y   •   F   O   U   R

The message of the Gospel is fairly simple, as John puts it:

> And this is eternal life, that they know You the only true
> God, and Jesus Christ whom You have sent. (John 17:3)

How can you be part of communicating this message to a friend or family member who has not heard?

And in Jesus Christ . . .

In the Large Catechism, Luther summarized the Second Article of the Creed with these words:

> Let this, then, be the sum of this article: the little word *Lord* means simply the same as *redeemer*. It means the One who has brought us from Satan to God, from death to life, from sin to righteousness, and who preserves us in the same.
> (Large Catechism, Part II, paragraph 31)

How would you summarize the life of Jesus Christ for someone who has never heard His story? What information is absolutely essential for this person to know?

In what creative ways could you communicate this essential information?

Notes

Heroes

Leon Jameson

Therefore be imitators of God, as beloved children. (Ephesians 5:1)

When I was seven, I got a Superman outfit for my birthday. I was so excited that I ran to my bedroom to change. First I pulled on the royal blue pants (Superman wears *pants* and not *tights*, thank you very much), and then the blue shirt with the red and yellow Superman emblem, and then the cape. That's when I saw it—a tag that said, "Warning: This is just a costume. Only Superman can fly."

A good warning. A warning probably intended for parents to read, but being a seven-year-old boy, I wanted to make sure. So I sneaked outside, climbed limb by limb into my favorite oak tree, carefully shimmied out onto a branch, and gave it the old Superman jump. You know the jump I'm talking about: the one-arm-out, one-leg-bent-under jump.

When I came to, I decided not to test the bullet thing.

My parents tell me that I wore my Superman costume everywhere: to the grocery store, to the bank, to the park, and even to school. One morning I even tried to wear it to church, but my mother drew the line. I remember people made fun of me, but I didn't care. Superman was my hero, and when you have a hero, you want to look like that person—no matter who laughs.

Heroes have always been an important part of my life. When I was thirteen, I loved watching cartoons that focused on heroes. In fact, I still watch cartoons today for the same reason, but now I have a convenient excuse. "No, honey, the baby wants to watch cartoons with Daddy; sorry, I can't take out the trash."

As teenagers, my best friend, Seth, and I shared a mutual appreciation for cartoons. Once a month or so, I would watch Saturday morning cartoons over at his house. Saturday morning cartoons at Seth's house were not spectator shows. After staying up late, we would get up early to watch *Teenage Mutant Ninja Turtles*. Without fail, after a few seconds of the opening theme song, Seth would "become" Michelangelo, swinging around the living room, jumping from chair to chair, swinging a set of nunchucks made from string and PVC pipe, and hollering, "*Cowabunga!*" Seth literally *became* Michelangelo; that was his hero. And when you have a hero, you want to look like that person—no matter what.

And since Seth was doing the casting, I got to be a foot soldier.

When I was a high school student, a real-life hero took center stage in my life. Tim was a Marine and a volunteer youth leader at our congregation. He was an absolutely huge guy, six feet seven, muscles like Hercules's, and a heart like a golden retriever's. His love for Jesus was also larger than life.

I have great memories of spending time with Tim during youth group. I remember the games we played, the food we ate, and the jokes we told. I remember being really impressed by the way Tim lived his faith; the way Tim prayed; and the intentionality of Tim's words when he was leading a Bible study. It wasn't too long before I wanted to be like this incredible man of God.

I remember hanging out during midweek Bible study at Tim's house and getting Tim's hat from the closet. I'd plop on the hat, which easily came to my nose, and I'd pull on his jacket, which hung to my knees. Then I'd put on his combat boots and walk around the house, pretending I was Tim.

The group always laughed; *I* always laughed. I looked so ridiculous when I tried on Tim's clothes. But in some ways, I wasn't playing dress-up. Because when you have a hero, you want to look like that person—no matter what.

It's been said that we should choose our heroes carefully because sooner or later, we'll resemble them.

As I look back on my relationship with Tim, I realize that he is still one of the most important influencers in my life. My life and attitude were changed by the way he imitated his hero, Jesus. Tim lived a life of service, not only to his country, but also to his church. Tim didn't just *speak* God's Word; he sought to model it in the way he lived his life. Tim was an imitator of Jesus, and that defined how he thought, talked, and acted.

Scripture tells us to be imitators of God and to walk, live, and love as Christ did. Other cross-references for this same passage tell us to be "perfect" even as our heavenly Father is perfect; to be kind and tenderhearted; to forgive as Christ forgave us; and to be merciful. When you have a hero, you want to look like that person—no matter what; and through God's Word, we are given a clear picture of how to be like Christ. Through His Spirit, we can model our life and our actions to really resemble Him.

Chances are, as you go through life, you'll meet someone who sees you the way I saw Tim. Here's what you want to do: make sure that when others see you and imitate you and try to be just like you, it's really Christ Jesus they imitate. In the end, that's really who Tim shared with me, and that's truly what made him the very best kind of hero.

Leon Jameson Minister to youth and families at Immanuel Lutheran Church in St. Charles, Missouri, Leon has been serving youth for over a decade now (yowza!) and seriously loves this calling. Leon speaks regularly to teenagers and adults throughout the United States. He is happiest when spending time with his wife, Gretchen, and eating the Play-Doh "food" creations of his two-year-old, Sydney Grace. When he is away from ministry, you can find Leon mowing his yard, playing tennis, wrestling his golden retriever, Bailey, collecting M&M candy dispensers, and eating German chocolate cake (hands down the greatest food on the planet). Leon's mission is to live for Jesus, leading others to do the same. Follow Leon on Facebook at: http://www.facebook.com/leon.jameson or on Twitter username: leonjameson.

His only Son, our Lord, who was conceived by the Holy Spirit, born of the Virgin Mary . . .

Leon really idolized his childhood heroes. Did you ever have similar childhood heroes? If so, what did you do to imitate them?

In his Letter to the Church at Ephesus, Paul encourages us to be imitators:

> Therefore be imitators of God, as beloved children. And walk in love, as Christ loved us and gave Himself up for us, a fragrant offering and sacrifice to God. (Ephesians 5:1–2).

What does it mean to be an imitator of God?

On your own, you could never imitate God. The world and your sinful nature battle against you from every side. But because Christ gave Himself up for you, you are already an imitator of Christ. In fact, the name you wear in faith—*Christian*—literally means "little Christ." In what other ways can you imitate Christ for those who don't yet know Him?

His only Son, our Lord, who was conceived by the Holy Spirit, born of the Virgin Mary . . .

Have you ever thought about why Jesus had to become human? Why did God the Father carry out this plan of action? In the Large Catechism, Martin Luther spends a lot of time discussing the Second Article of the Apostles' Creed and the work and role of Jesus Christ.

> Providing a sweeping description of Creation and the fall, Luther notes that the word *we* includes every single person in the horrible drama of the Garden of Eden. In that sin we all fell away from God and were doomed to everlasting damnation. Yet Christ, our Lord, came and snatched us from the jaws of hell. (Large Catechism, Part II, note on Article II)

We are all part of what happened in the Garden of Eden; Adam and Eve's sin sticks to us all. The "horrible drama," as it is called, seems like the scene from a nightmare. Read Genesis 3 again and try to imagine how a horror movie producer might replay this story today.

Fortunately for us, the story doesn't end there. We are literally snatched from the jaws of hell through the suffering, death, and resurrection of our Lord and Savior, Jesus Christ.

Think about the drama of your salvation, and outline how you might retell the story in a creative way for other young people.

His only Son, our Lord, who was conceived by the Holy Spirit, born of the Virgin Mary . . .

D A Y • T H R E E

> Jesus' work of reversing the worldly order begins at His birth and culminates with His death on the cross. By His incarnation and death, Jesus puts fallen creation back into the realm of the magnificent. His life is God's great reversal. (*TLSB*, p. 1705)

The work of Jesus Christ is often called "the great reversal." His life and ministry ran counter to what many expected. Jesus gave up His heavenly glory to take the form of a man. He preached peace rather than warfare. Jesus had no need or desire for earthly fame and glory. He allowed Himself to be tortured and killed for our sake. What other "great reversal" examples from the life of Christ do you recall?

What other individuals do you know who have experienced a personal great reversal because of Christ's great reversal? Write their stories as you journal today.

His only Son, our Lord, who was conceived by the Holy Spirit, born of the Virgin Mary . . .

From the days of the Old Testament prophets, the children of Israel awaited the coming of the Savior. The great prophet Isaiah wrote:

> Therefore the Lord Himself will give you a sign. Behold, the virgin shall conceive and bear a son, and shall call His name Immanuel. (Isaiah 7:14)

Yet, when the Fulfillment of this prophecy came, God's chosen people rejected Him. How do people today reject the One called "Immanuel"?

How might you at times fail to recognize Him?

But there is good news, even when we falter: "If we are faithless, He remains faithful" (2 Timothy 2:13). Write a prayer thanking God for His faithfulness.

His only Son, our Lord, who was conceived by the Holy Spirit, born of the Virgin Mary . . .

And the angel said to her, "Do not be afraid, Mary, for you have found favor with God. And behold, you will conceive in your womb and bear a son, and you shall call His name Jesus. He will be great and will be called the Son of the Most High. And the Lord God will give to Him the throne of His father David, and He will reign over the house of Jacob forever, and of His kingdom there will be no end."

And Mary said to the angel, "How will this be, since I am a virgin?"

And the angel answered her, "The Holy Spirit will come upon you, and the power of the Most High will overshadow you; therefore the child to be born will be called holy—the Son of God." (Luke 1:30–35)

Mary could scarcely believe the angel's announcement. Unmarried and pregnant, she faced potentially dangerous consequences. Yet she faithfully accepted the task given her:

"My soul magnifies the Lord,
   and my spirit rejoices in God my Savior,
   for He has looked on the humble estate of His servant.
For behold, from now on all generations will call me blessed;
   for He who is mighty has done great things for me,
   and holy is His name." (Luke 1:46–49)

How can you rejoice in the face of difficult tasks? What resources has God given you to face these challenges?

Notes

Scents

Alaina Kleinbeck

In the backyard of my childhood home, we had a lilac bush the size of a small country. Every year in the late spring, it stunk up the whole neighborhood with its syrupy sweet aroma. We'd shake the overgrown branches and let the tiny flowers fall like confetti onto our hair and our clothes, carpeting the ground.

When I go running in the late spring, I sometimes breathe in wafts of lilac. Its potent scent reminds me of a simpler time, a time when emptying the dishwasher was the only thing that interrupted my endless book reading, bike rides, and backyard explorations. Lilac smells like childhood joy, uncomplicated by the murkier parts of life.

The murky parts crashed into my life like the rising tide on a beach blanket. I was days away from beginning high school when my little brother was in a bicycle accident, the kind of accident that kills people instantly. But my brother was wearing a helmet, and he lived long enough for us to collect a few days' worth of nightmarish memories. When it was finally over, we were able to donate his organs so that other families might not have to continue in their nightmares.

I can't think about those days without feeling like someone chopped down the lilac bush from our backyard and left it to decompose. Their memory lingers like a rotten pile of garbage with its stench and rats and flies. For my parents, my older sister, and me, my brother's death brought deep grief, persistent depression, and anger at a God who would tear apart our family.

My family was the churchgoing type. We grew up attending Sunday School, Vacation Bible School, confirmation classes, and then youth group. My mom led Christmas programs and Sunday School. My dad served in church leadership. We prayed before mealtimes. Sometimes we talked about our faith. But after my brother died, no one felt like getting out of bed on Sunday morning. Church was the place we had said goodbye, and every song seemed to make my mom cry. Whenever someone mentioned that my brother was in heaven, I felt like asking if they wanted their brother to trade places with mine. It was easier to stay at home than to sit through that torture. Over time, I quietly decided that I either didn't believe that God existed or that I was angry enough to ignore Him for the rest of my life.

I still posed as a believer. I couldn't put my mom through that misery, and I didn't want my pastor to bother me with six hundred questions. It was easier to pose than to deal with the dark parts of my heart. I'd been given the opportunity to serve in a couple of leadership positions through church. I thought it would look good on college applications. The gods of a shining college application spoke loudly.

Determined to escape from my grief and my poser-induced exhaustion, I decided that I needed to become a foreign-exchange student. My parents were driving me crazy, and I probably was driving them crazy. Becoming a foreign-exchange student was the easiest way to run away from home without dealing with the police. Besides, I knew that a year in Spain would look good on the ever-looming college application.

Living in Spain was challenging for all of the obvious reasons of language and culture. My friends in Madrid were diverse: Buddhist, atheist, non-practicing Catholics, Communist Party members, children of hippies. They were nothing like my Christian friends from rural Missouri. Their diversity excited me. And though it struck me that something was different about my faith experience, I was determined not to talk about faith.

One day, I was working on a project with a fellow exchange student, Thomas. He looked me straight in the eye and said, "I don't think people have the capability to love. They are self-serving by design. They may say 'I love you,' but they are only looking for what they will get in return." His words hung in the air for several long moments before I had a chance to unfurrow my eyebrows. Sure, I hated a lot about my life and my parents and my brother dying and how no one seemed to get how much it all hurt, but I knew without a doubt that my parents loved me and my sister and each other. Life couldn't be so empty like he said. Love was something that I believed in.

And so I defended love with everything I knew. Words poured out of my mouth.

Love wasn't just a word that a guy says to a girl when he wants that something he shouldn't.

Love was self-sacrifice:

⇨ Two people staying married when one of them asks every day if they have to get out of bed and face the day
⇨ A parent setting aside personal needs to care for a child endlessly
⇨ A pastor sitting with a family in the hospital for hours and days on end, holding their hands while they watch their loved one die
⇨ A Father giving up His Son to save a people from their rotting piles of broken hearts and broken lives

Love was something I believed in.

As I talked, it hit me that I was talking about Christ's sacrifice on the cross. I didn't know it at the time, but I was fumbling around Jesus' words in John 15:13: "Greater love has no one than this, that someone lay down his life for his friends." All of my experiences with love were born out of God's example of love for His people, for my parents, for my sister, for me. I'd experienced sacrificial love from my parents, and so love had to exist. So then, somehow, mysteriously, so did a God whose sacrificial love led Him to death.

Losing my brother still feels like a rotting pile of lilac branches. It still hurts, but since the day I spoke to Thomas about love, the rot and pain aren't the only things I see. I don't see God as the Creator of pain, but as the Redeemer from pain. He has shown me that His love isn't dependent on a beautiful, flowering tree or on a life that produces shining college applications. He sent Jesus to pull me from my murky, rotting piles and from my need to be perfect.

He has taken the rot and brokenness from my life and planted hope in Christ in me. My life through Christ is a new creation, a new lilac tree, a place of hope in darkness (2 Corinthians 5:17). I, the grieving poser girl, am a new creation because of Christ's great, life-laying-down love. The new lilac tree is bigger, bushier, and stinkier—all the better to loudly shout Christ's love for me.

Alaina Kleinbeck Alaina works with middle school students at a church in suburban St. Louis. She likes chocolate, U2, and listening to NPR. She dreams of returning to Spain, learning how to flamenco dance, and sharing her faith with the people there. Check out Alaina's blog at: http://kleinbeck.blogspot.com/ or follow her tweets on Twitter username: kleinbeck.

... suffered under Pontius Pilate, was crucified, died and was buried.

Alaina's faith story shares a real crisis in faith prompted by the death of her brother. Have you ever suffered the loss of a close friend or family member? How did that person's death affect you?

As Christians, we understand that death is not the end for the believer. Through faith, we inherit Christ's victory over sin, death, and the devil.

> He did none of these things for Himself, nor did He have any need for redemption. After that He rose again from the dead, swallowed up and devoured death, and finally ascended into heaven and assumed the government at the Father's right hand. He did these things so that the devil and all powers must be subject to Him and lie at His feet. (Large Catechism, Part II, paragraph 31)

As you journal today, write a prayer of thanksgiving to God for your victory in Jesus Christ.

... suffered under Pontius Pilate, was crucified, died and was buried.

Imagine yourself as one of the disciples watching the following scene. How might you react?

> Then Pilate took Jesus and flogged Him. And the soldiers twisted together a crown of thorns and put it on His head and arrayed Him in a purple robe. They came up to Him, saying, "Hail, King of the Jews!" and struck Him with their hands. (John 19:1–3)

The suffering Jesus endured at the hands of Pilate and the Roman soldiers seems unimaginable. The reason for that suffering is even more unreal: it's *your* fault!

Why did Jesus allow Himself to be beaten and killed? For you!

. . . suffered under Pontius Pilate, was crucified, died and was buried.

In the Book of Concord (a collection of confessional statements), there is a section entitled "Catalog of Testimonies." This catalog contains a number of one- and two-sentence summaries of the Christian faith. One of these testimonies reads:

> If anyone does not confess that the Word of God suffered in the flesh, was crucified in the flesh, and tasted death in the flesh, becoming the firstborn from the dead, although as God He is life and gives life, let him be accursed. (Book of Concord: Catalog of Testimonies, Canon 12)

Wow! This is some strong language! Why do you suppose the writers of this testimony used such powerful words?

... suffered under Pontius Pilate, was crucified, died and was buried.

The Old Testament prophet Isaiah foretold the suffering and death of Jesus Christ:

> Surely He has borne our griefs
>   and carried our sorrows;
> yet we esteemed Him stricken,
>   smitten by God, and afflicted.
> But He was wounded for our transgressions;
>   He was crushed for our iniquities;
> upon Him was the chastisement that brought us peace,
>   and with His stripes we are healed.
> All we like sheep have gone astray;
>   we have turned—every one—to his own way;
> and the LORD has laid on Him
>   the iniquity of us all.
>
> He was oppressed, and He was afflicted,
>   yet He opened not His mouth;
> like a lamb that is led to the slaughter,
>   and like a sheep that before its shearers is silent,
>   so He opened not His mouth.
> By oppression and judgment He was taken away;
>   and as for His generation, who considered
> that He was cut off out of the land of the living,
>   stricken for the transgression of My people?
> And they made His grave with the wicked
>   and with a rich man in His death,
> although He had done no violence,
>   and there was no deceit in His mouth.
>
> Yet it was the will of the LORD to crush Him;
>   He has put Him to grief. (Isaiah 53:4–10)

Select one or two verses from Isaiah's prophecy and write a brief devotional prayer based on those words.

... suffered under Pontius Pilate, was crucified, died and was buried.

So they took Jesus, and He went out, bearing His own cross, to the place called The Place of a Skull, which in Aramaic is called Golgotha. There they crucified Him, and with Him two others, one on either side, and Jesus between them. (John 19:16–18)

In these short verses, John summarizes the events of Good Friday. As Christians, we know the story doesn't end here. In the space below, tell in your own words how the story ends.

Notes

Shame

Reed Lessing

Rob Poulos is a walking piece of literature. He has tattooed on his left wrist, "B-A-C-K" with a period. It looks as though it was lifted from the end of a sentence. It was.

A few years ago, Poulos joined a worldwide effort to help author Shelley Jackson tell her story on people's bodies. Appropriately titled *Skin*, the "book" has 2,095 words. Each person bears on his or her or body just one word.

The prophet Isaiah also envisions people marked with one word. He writes, "Another will write on his hand, *'leyahweh'*" (Isaiah 44:5). *Leyahweh* is one word in Hebrew that in English means, "belonging to the LORD."

When I was in high school, I was marked with another word: *shame*. No, I didn't have it tattooed on my body; it was worse than that. Shame was engraved upon my heart.

Don't confuse shame with regret. Very often, regret has a redeeming quality to it. You see, without regret, we are unable to repent of our sins, seek forgiveness, and receive the free gift of the Father's grace in Christ. To a large extent, feelings of regret and remorse teach us about humility and our need for Jesus' mercy.

On the other hand, shame has no such redeeming qualities. When shame is etched upon our hearts, we don't *make* mistakes; we feel as though we *are* mistakes. Shame is feeling bad not because of something we've *done*, but because of *who we are*.

Shame left its mark on me every time I compared myself with other kids in my high school. There was Larry Lillo, who was an all-state quarterback. At five *feet* nine inches and 135 pounds, let's just say that *my* football career was over before it ever got started. There was Brent Singer, who got straight A's. I was in the top 10 percent of my class, but colleges didn't court *me* and claim *me* with first-class academic scholarships. And then there was Tim Dennis. Tim always seemed to have three or four cute girls vying for his attention. And me? I had one date in high school.

High school students have limitless opportunities to feel shame. It seems as though classrooms are filled with "experts" who shame us about our looks, our music, our hobbies, our parents, and our friends (or lack thereof). The list could go on and on.

And so I was overwhelmed with *D* words—*depressed, defeated, defective, deficient, deserted, diminished, desperate, devastated,* and *diminished.* But one word summed up my life: *shame.*

How about you? Do you

⇨ feel unsatisfied with how you look, no matter how many compliments you get?

⇨ allow yourself to be abused verbally, physically, or even sexually?

⇨ feel like a failure, no matter how successful you are?

⇨ feel unsure of your opinions and reluctant to express them?

Shame is not something that comes upon us all at once. In most cases, it is inflicted over and over again—either maliciously or inadvertently—by parents, friends, and authority figures such as coaches and teachers. Then, at some point, we become not only *victims* but *perpetrators* of shame, as we pick up where others left off and begin to shame ourselves.

In league with these forces of shame is Satan's strategy of damaging us further. We are called "beloved" by God in Holy Baptism, but the devil calls us "cheap," "dirty," and "worthless." We are deemed washed and cleansed by the blood of Jesus, but Satan whispers to us, "Guilty as charged." We are designated as "a chosen race, a royal priesthood, a holy nation, a people for His own possession" (1 Peter 2:9), but the liar brazenly boasts, "You will never amount to anything!"

I was easy prey for the devil until I heard in college that I could be marked with another word—a word that frees and forgives, a word that lifts and loves. It is the word the prophet writes about in Isaiah 44:5: "Another will write on his hand, *leyahweh*." Wonder of wonders, I was told that Jesus loves me and that, baptized in the name of the Father, Son, and Holy Spirit, "belonging to the LORD" was now emblazoned upon my forehead and upon my heart!

God has always told His story on people's bodies, call it *Skin*! In Genesis 4:15, He graciously marks Cain, and in Genesis 17:1–14, He gives Abraham and his offspring the covenant mark of circumcision. Deuteronomy 6:8 describes people tying the Lord's words on their hands and binding them on their foreheads, while in Ezekiel 9:4, God commands a man with a writing kit to go throughout the city of Jerusalem and put a mark of protection on the foreheads of those who grieve over all the detestable things that are done in the city.

And all this points to the most awesome story ever told on human skin. Isaiah describes the body with these words:

> His appearance was so marred, beyond human semblance, and His form beyond that of the children of mankind. . . . He was despised and rejected by men; a man of sorrows, and acquainted with grief; and as one from whom men hide their faces, He was despised, and we esteemed Him not. . . . But He was wounded for our transgressions; He was crushed for our iniquities; upon Him was the chastise-

ment that brought us peace, and with His stripes we are healed. (Isaiah 52:14; 53:3, 5)

One spear, three nails, and a crown of thorns left their marks on Jesus; did they ever!

But Jesus' disciples saw Him alive—and Jesus still had His marks (John 20:20–29). Jesus is alive, and He is forever marked with scars announcing His loyal love and His free forgiveness and His grace gone wild!

And so people began lining up to be marked. Paul puts it this way in Galatians 6:17: "I bear on my body the marks of Jesus." Bodies marked with Jesus have eyes full of tenderness and kindness, hands full of compassion and care, and mouths full of joy and love!

To be a part of this story of salvation, all we need to take on is one word in Hebrew, *leyahweh*; or four words in English, "belonging to the LORD."

But just how does that happen? Remember your Baptism and never forget these words connected to it: "Receive the sign of the holy cross, both upon your forehead and upon your heart *to mark you* as one redeemed by Christ the crucified."

In Holy Baptism, our *shame* is erased, and in its place, the most powerful word in heaven or on earth is forever imprinted upon our hearts—*Jesus*!

Reed Lessing Born and raised in the Mile High City of Denver, Colorado, Reed loves his wife, Lisa, and their three children, Abi, Jonathan, and Lori. Each of these adorable Lessing children has participated in past LCMS National Youth Gatherings. Reed faithfully roots for the St. Louis Cardinals, has jogged over fifty thousand miles in the last thirty years, and is continually fascinated by the best language on the planet, Hebrew! You can keep up with Reed on Facebook at: http://www.facebook.com/reedlessing.

The third day He rose again from the dead.

The Large Catechism summarizes the work of Jesus Christ with these words:

> For when we had been created by God the Father and had received from Him all kinds of good, the devil came and led us into disobedience, sin, death, and all evil. So we fell under God's wrath and displeasure and were doomed to eternal damnation, just as we had merited and deserved. There was no counsel, help, or comfort until this only and eternal Son of God—in His immeasurable goodness—had compassion upon our misery and wretchedness. He came from heaven to help us. So those tyrants and jailers are all expelled now. In their place has come Jesus Christ, Lord of life, righteousness, every blessing, and salvation. He has delivered us poor, lost people from hell's jaws, has won us, has made us free, and has brought us again into the Father's favor and grace. He has taken us as His own property under His shelter and protection so that He may govern us by His righteousness, wisdom, power, life, and blessedness. (Large Catechism, Part II, paragraphs 28–30)

How would you summarize the work of Jesus?

The third day He rose again from the dead.

The Augsburg Confession also contains a summary of Jesus' life, death, and resurrection:

> Our churches teach that the Word, that is, the Son of God, assumed the human nature in the womb of the Blessed Virgin Mary. So there are two natures—the divine and the human—inseparably joined in one person. There is one Christ, true God and true man, who was born of the Virgin Mary, truly suffered, was crucified, died, and was buried. He did this to reconcile the Father to us and to be a sacrifice, not only for original guilt, but also for all actual sins of mankind.

> He also descended into hell, and truly rose again on the third day. Afterward, He ascended into heaven to sit at the right hand of the Father. There He forever reigns and has dominion over all creatures. He sanctifies those who believe in Him, by sending the Holy Spirit into their hearts to rule, comfort, and make them alive. He defends them against the devil and the power of sin.

> The same Christ will openly come again to judge the living and the dead, and so forth, according to the Apostles' Creed. (Augsburg Confession, Article III, paragraphs 1–6)

How does this compare with the Large Catechism version you read yesterday? How are they different? How are they the same?

Why do you suppose there are these differences?

The third day He rose again from the dead.

D A Y • T H R E E

> For I delivered to you as of first importance what I also received: that Christ died for our sins in accordance with the Scriptures, that He was buried, that He was raised on the third day in accordance with the Scriptures, and that He appeared to Cephas, then to the twelve. (1 Corinthians 15:3–5)

Later in this chapter Paul refers to himself as "one untimely born" (v. 8; the NIV says "abnormally born"). He did not fully see or understand the work of Christ until he met the risen Christ on the road to Damascus. Paul would spend the rest of his life proclaiming the message of Christ to the world.

Who do you know that needs to hear the message of Christ? How might you help them hear that message?

The third day He rose again from the dead.

> But God raised Him on the third day and made Him to appear, not to all the people but to us who had been chosen by God as witnesses, who ate and drank with Him after He rose from the dead. (Acts 10:40–41)

Jesus' followers ate and drank with Him following the resurrection. Many of them would die for sharing the Easter message. What opportunities for witnessing the Easter message has God put in your life?

The third day He rose again from the dead.

D A Y • F I V E

What is your most special or favorite Easter memory? Why is that memory important to you?

Notes

PK
Ryan Peterson

I used to think my journey of faith was boring, common, and not very interesting. Who knows . . . after reading this, you may feel the same way about my journey. But I've come to realize that it's *my* journey, not someone else's. It doesn't involve drugs. It doesn't involve alcohol. It doesn't even involve sex. But it does involve a life of getting to know Jesus.

For as long as I can recall, I have been a follower of Jesus. I was baptized as an infant, grew up in the Church, attended a Lutheran grade school and a Lutheran high school, and then went on to a Lutheran university. Some people would say that kind of journey was sheltered and not a good example of "the real world."

You see, I was often called "the teacher's pet" or some other flattering name. I was a pretty good student, a decent athlete, and a socially outgoing kid. Most of that stayed with me through my high school years ("decent athlete" might be a stretch, though).

I don't know why my life has gone the way it has, or what the future holds for me, but I do know that journeys with God are rarely boring, common, or uninteresting. No matter what your journey has been, remember that there is a lot along the journey that will change or challenge you. I've had my share of both.

The summer between eighth grade and my freshman year of high school was life changing. My dad was a successful businessman who co-owned Stewart-Peterson Advisory Group (guess which one he was) in West Bend, Wisconsin. He traveled occasionally, but not that often. This summer, though, he and my mom took a three-week business trip to various states around the country. When they arrived back home, we had a "family meeting." You know those types of meetings, right? Usually something big happens.

And it did.

As we gathered in our downstairs recreation room, my dad shared how he and my mom would sell our family's half of the business, and my dad would start graduate work at Concordia Seminary in St. Louis, Missouri. In other words, my dad was going to move from businessman to pastor, and he felt total peace about that huge decision.

Some of your dads are pastors. Now, so is mine. But I never considered myself a "pastor's kid" while growing up.

So how did this impact my faith journey, what I believed, and what I held to be true about life, God, and my relationships?

It messed with *everything.*

I used to think the goal of life was fame, success, knowledge, and popularity. Along with that, then, would come money, opportunity, and a big house with a pool in the backyard. Suddenly, the one person I looked to more than anyone else in the world was willing to move into a tiny dorm room, eat out of a cafeteria, and travel back and forth from Wisconsin to St. Louis *weekly* so that he wouldn't miss out on any of our high school activities. He was obedient to God's call in his life. He didn't run away. He didn't hide. He followed. He followed with an open heart and a willing spirit.

And in the midst of that entire process, I saw God's faithfulness. I saw His promise that "He will not leave you or forsake you" (Deuteronomy 31:6). I loved high school. But it's hard to go through it alone. I never did, because as long as Jesus was living inside me (Galatians 2:20), I knew I would never be alone.

It's hard to describe in words how my dad's example shaped my life. At the family meeting, I remember, one of my siblings asked, "Does this mean we're going to be poor now?" It crossed my mind, but I never said it. We were never poor. In fact, God used that moment to open my heart more to Him and more to the needs of the people around me.

That same summer between eighth grade and freshman year, a man I really looked up to said something I'll never forget: "Ryan, from everyone who has been given much, much will be expected." That saying has summed up so much of my journey. Jesus said something like that, didn't He?

This man, whom I respect even to this day, echoed something Jesus said two thousand years ago. His words are for all of us. There's a great burden of responsibility and privilege that God gives to so many people, myself included.

Your identity is not found in your grade point average, your athletic ability, or the number of friends you have on Facebook. I used to think that way. In fact, throughout high school, and even during the moments I have described here, I fought against the truth of my real identity. It's something I struggle with still today. It's easy for me, a driven, type-A person, to find comfort in accomplishment, encouragement, and status.

Someone once said, "People need to be reminded more than instructed." If your story is anything like mine, I think that's true and probably helpful for you to remember.

Life is about counting on the promises of God. I need to be reminded of those promises all the time. Otherwise, I go on autopilot and end up putting my identity in stuff. God promises that He will never leave me; that Jesus is the way, the truth, and the life; and that my eternity is secure because of Jesus' life, death, and resurrection for my sake.

Ryan Peterson Ryan Peterson is one of the pastors at St. John in Ellisville, Missouri. He loves the adventures and challenges of being a husband, dad, and pastor. Every day he tries to figure out more about each of these unique roles in life. When he's not running or biking, Ryan enjoys a great cup of coffee (he *loves* Starbucks!) and a good book. He has been married to his beautiful Kristy for seven years, and God has given them two cool boys—Andrew and Kyle. You'll find Ryan posting status updates on Facebook and Twitter. His Twitter username is ryanSTLSTL.

He ascended into heaven and sits at the right hand of God. . . . From thence He will come to judge the living and the dead.

In Jesus, God's salvation has come *now*. It is here *today*. God's people, and indeed all creation, enjoy the blessings of redemption. The joy of being with God eternally is already here for us in the Word and Sacrament ministry of the Church (called "inaugurated eschatology"). *Yet*, we still await Jesus' final reappearing when He will come again to judge the living and the dead and complete the work of His kingdom. (*TLSB*, p. 1701)

Christians are often heard saying that they long for heaven. They desire to leave this sinful world for an eternity with Christ. But as this quote clearly points out, as redeemed children of God, we already live in the presence of God. We live in the "now and not yet."

In what ways are you already connected to your Savior?

He ascended into heaven and sits at the right hand of God. . . . From thence He will come to judge the living and the dead.

D A Y • T W O

Each of us has been given a walk-on role in the divine drama of salvation, but the Lord Himself remains the actor with top billing. He acts in us, through us, and for us, even to the end of the age. (*TLSB*, p. 1841)

Have you ever thought about your life of faith in this way? What is your walk-on role?

How is the Lord using you in the divine drama?

He ascended into heaven and sits at the right hand of God. . . . From thence He will come to judge the living and the dead.

So what exactly is Jesus doing in heaven? The Lutheran Confessions teach:

> Now He has ascended to heaven, not merely as any other saint, but as the apostle testifies, above all heavens. He also truly fills all things, being present everywhere, not only as God, but also as man. He rules from sea to sea and to the ends of the earth, as the prophets predict and the apostles testify. He did this everywhere with them and confirmed their word with signs. This did not happen in an earthly way. . . . This happened according to the way things are done at God's right hand. "God's right hand" is no set place in heaven. . . . It is nothing other than God's almighty power, which fills heaven and earth. (Solid Declaration of the Formula of Concord, Article VIII, paragraphs 27–28)

What does it mean for you that Jesus sits at God's right hand? Why is this important?

He ascended into heaven and sits at the right hand of God. . . . From thence He will come to judge the living and the dead.

D A Y • F O U R

He worked in Christ when He raised Him from the dead and seated Him at His right hand in the heavenly places, far above all rule and authority and power and dominion, and above every name that is named, not only in this age but also in the one to come. And He put all things under His feet and gave Him as head over all things to the church. (Ephesians 1:20–22)

What does this scene described in Paul's Letter to the Church at Ephesus bring to mind? Describe it in your own words or draw it during your journal time today.

He ascended into heaven and sits at the right hand of God. . . . From thence He will come to judge the living and the dead.

And when He had said these things, as they were looking on, He was lifted up, and a cloud took Him out of their sight. And while they were gazing into heaven as He went, behold, two men stood by them in white robes, and said, "Men of Galilee, why do you stand looking into heaven? This Jesus, who was taken up from you into heaven, will come in the same way as you saw Him go into heaven." (Acts 1:9–11)

The disciples stood in awe as Jesus disappeared from view into heaven. In the same way, all humanity will stand in fear and awe at His reappearance.

Behold, He is coming with the clouds, and every eye will see Him, even those who pierced Him, and all tribes of the earth will wail on account of Him. Even so. Amen. (Revelation 1:7)

What will your reaction be on the Last Day? What about your family and friends?

Notes

Full Circle

Tony Boos

As I was grow-ing up, my mother would often recount a story about my earliest days, when I was being raised in the jungle in a nipa-thatched hut in the Philippines. An exciting Filipino cus-tom happens when a baby first learns to crawl. The family places different objects in front of the child to see which one the baby will grab first. That object is said to indicate the baby's future vocation. For example, if a baby grabs a pencil, it will grow up to work in business; if the baby picks up a tool, he'll be a farmer or carpenter; if it's flowers, she'll marry early; and if it's a rosary or crucifix, the child will serve God as a Catholic priest or nun. Guess which one I grabbed? The crucifix! Pretty wild, considering I am a pastor now! So, in the summer of 1967, my Nanay and Tatay (grandma and grandpa) gleefully announced, "Antonio is going to be a priest!" But whether or not I had become an ordained priest/pastor, *all* Christians are actually the "royal priesthood" in God's eyes. The Bible says, "But you are a cho-sen race, a royal priesthood, a holy nation, a people for His own possession, that you may proclaim the excellencies of Him who called you out of darkness into His marvelous light" (1 Peter 2:9).

Well, I didn't exactly take those first crawls right to serv-ing God full time. Despite the fact that I attended Mass every Sunday during my elementary and high school years, I truly had no idea what Jesus' death and resurrection meant for my life. I didn't have a relationship with Him. It wasn't until I began college and met a cute, blond, German Lutheran girl that I started to understand the difference between a religion and a relationship with Jesus. She asked me quite simply, "What do you think of Jesus?"

My response to her (which I'll never forget) was, "What do you mean?! I go to church several times a week, and right now it's Lent, so I'm fasting from meat!" I didn't even answer her question about Jesus! To me, it was all about what *I was doing* that my religion stipulated would please God.

As my college years went on, I never gave a thought about Jesus. My concerns were girls, soccer, and having fun. It was all about *me* and no one else. Looking back on those years, I am still amazed at how merciful God was to me! I often thank God for sparing my life—I could have died, what with all the idiotic stunts I pulled and the thoughtless choices I made. It wasn't until my relationship deepened with the Lutheran girl who had asked me that poignant question and we were on the verge of a breakup that I began to personally talk to God: "Why is this happening, God? Will I lose her forever?"

For several years, she was away at a state college; I eventually graduated and began my life in the work force. I started attending a nondenominational singles Bible study with a friend. I was twenty-one years old, and for the first time in my life, I opened God's Word for myself. I wasn't just being in church, listening to a priest talk to me about God. It was through this personal study that I realized the most amazing gift I had ever received in my life—Baptism! Although all my days so far had been spent not thinking about or caring about Jesus, He was always thinking about and caring for me. Our almighty and merciful God, through His Word and the Holy Spirit, allowed me a greater understanding of the wonderful gift given to me at my Baptism as an infant in the Philippines.

Turns out that the blond, blue-eyed Lutheran girl is now my wife of sixteen years. Through our relationship, I was brought to the most important relationship anyone could ever have—a relationship with my Lord and Savior, Jesus! No more religion for me; now I was in a relationship with God Himself.

I eagerly joined a Lutheran church in 1992, and during my adult confirmation process, I was taught Luther's Catechism. I will never forget two important teachings. The first comes from the Explanation of the Third Article of the Apostles' Creed: "I believe that I cannot by my own reason or strength believe in Jesus Christ, my Lord, or come to Him; but the Holy Spirit has called me by the Gospel, enlightened me with His gifts, sanctified and kept me in the true faith." When I read this, Jesus came alive in a way never before explained to me. There was nothing I could do to try to please a holy God—that is only "religion," man's attempt at working toward God. However, I had had a relationship since the beginning of my life with the One who promised He would never leave me. I chose to walk away from Him for a time; yet, through the circumstances of my life, God in His mercy brought me to His life-giving Word to restore my faith. As 1 Thessalonians 1:4-5 says, "For we know, brothers loved by God, that He has chosen you, because our gospel came to you not only in word, but also in power and in the Holy Spirit and with full conviction."

The second memorable teaching from my Lutheran confirmation classes was related to how we need the Holy Spirit to begin and sustain faith in us. It struck me as I learned how, by nature, we are so absolutely spiritually blind, dead, and enemies of God. It amazed me that at my Baptism as a helpless infant, I received God's grace (unmerited favor) and was freely given faith to trust in Jesus. God began a relationship with me at my Baptism, and He brought me back to Himself as an adult.

Now, it is my honor to serve Him full time as a pastor. It is such a privilege to be used by God to give His gift of Baptism to others. I'm sure glad I didn't grab for a pencil or tool on that first day of crawling!

Tony Boos Tony Boos does life with his wife and six children (ages 5–13) as an outreach pastor in Troy, Michigan (a suburb of Detroit). His passion is spreading the Gospel to the seventy-plus ethnic groups who live in his neighborhood. His next passion is soccer—playing, coaching his kids, watching. He is pretty sure he is the only Filipino LCMS pastor in the United States.

I believe in the Holy Spirit . . .

The Holy Spirit is probably the least understood Person of the Trinity, yet His work is essential in creating and sustaining faith. This week's journaling activities will focus on the person and work of the Holy Spirit. The Holy Spirit works through the words of Scripture:

> Through the Word He reveals and preaches, He illumines and enkindles hearts, so that they understand, accept, cling to, and persevere in the Word. (Large Catechism, Part 2, paragraph 42)

Contemplate some of your favorite words of Scripture. What are those words?
How do those words help you persevere in the world today?

I believe in the Holy Spirit . . .

D   A   Y   •   T   W   O

The psalmist reminds us that the Spirit of God is always with us:
> Where shall I go from Your Spirit?
>> Or where shall I flee from Your presence?
> If I ascend to heaven, You are there!
>> If I make my bed in Sheol, You are there!
> If I take the wings of the morning
>> and dwell in the uttermost parts of the sea,
> even there Your hand shall lead me,
>> and Your right hand shall hold me. (Psalm 139:7–10)

What comfort do these words offer to you as a believer?

In your journaling today, write about a time when you especially needed and felt the presence of God's Spirit.

I believe in the Holy Spirit . . .

D A Y • T H R E E

The Holy Spirit calls us to faith. In Revelation we see this action played out as the Spirit and the Bride (the Church) call out to the lost:

> "The Spirit and the Bride say, 'Come!' And let the one who hears say, 'Come!' And let the one who is thirsty come; let the one who desires take the water of life without price" (Revelation 22:17).

Consider how the Spirit first called you. Was it at your Baptism as an infant or some time later? Write what you know about that part of your faith story.

I believe in the Holy Spirit . . .

These things God has revealed to us through the Spirit. For the Spirit searches everything, even the depths of God. For who knows a person's thoughts except the spirit of that person, which is in him? So also no one comprehends the thoughts of God except the Spirit of God. Now we have received not the spirit of the world, but the Spirit who is from God, that we might understand the things freely given us by God. And we impart this in words not taught by human wisdom but taught by the Spirit, interpreting spiritual truths to those who are spiritual. The natural person does not accept the things of the Spirit of God, for they are folly to him, and he is not able to understand them because they are spiritually discerned. (1 Corinthians 2:10–14)

Through the Spirit, we are enabled to understand the things of God. Yet, this side of heaven, our understanding is flawed and incomplete. What do you not fully understand?

How could you gain the understanding you need?

I believe in the Holy Spirit . . .

There is therefore now no condemnation for those who are in Christ Jesus. For the law of the Spirit of life has set you free in Christ Jesus from the law of sin and death. For God has done what the law, weakened by the flesh, could not do. By sending His own Son in the likeness of sinful flesh and for sin, He condemned sin in the flesh, in order that the righteous requirement of the law might be fulfilled in us, who walk not according to the flesh but according to the Spirit. For those who live according to the flesh set their minds on the things of the flesh, but those who live according to the Spirit set their minds on the things of the Spirit. For to set the mind on the flesh is death, but to set the mind on the Spirit is life and peace. For the mind that is set on the flesh is hostile to God, for it does not submit to God's law; indeed, it cannot. Those who are in the flesh cannot please God.

You, however, are not in the flesh but in the Spirit, if in fact the Spirit of God dwells in you. Anyone who does not have the Spirit of Christ does not belong to Him. But if Christ is in you, although the body is dead because of sin, the Spirit is life because of righteousness. If the Spirit of Him who raised Jesus from the dead dwells in you, He who raised Christ Jesus from the dead will also give life to your mortal bodies through His Spirit who dwells in you. (Romans 8:1–11)

As you journal today, summarize Romans 8:1–11 in your own words.

Notes

Belong

Jeff Cloeter

I was rumored to stand six feet eight inches and weigh 230 pounds. It was whispered in the school hallways that I was a hoops phenom from Detroit. A tale was told that Duke was recruiting me and that North Carolina and Indiana were trying to edge in. Gossip soon became mythical legend: I had a shoe deal with Nike and an agent in L. A. I was a new kid, moving to a new high school during the summer after my sophomore year. And my legend grew, *all before the student body had ever met me.*

The legend became laughter when they found out I was actually a tall, skinny six feet *three* inches. I was in fact from Michigan, but not from the urban playgrounds of Detroit. I was from Bessemer, a remote logging town nestled in the rugged hills of the Upper Peninsula. And was I a hoops phenom? While I loved basketball, I possessed reasonably moderate skills—enough to compete, but certainly not to dominate.

The first day at my new school was marked by sweaty armpits and the feeling of a wrench in my gut. I was entering my junior year living in a new state, in an unfamiliar town, and walking the halls of an alien school. My class had grown from 43 to 343. And all 343 students knew that I was the mythical "Air Jordan" figure whose hype was mostly hot air. I stared at unfamiliar faces as I roamed the endless hallways, hunting for my locker. The school had the sterile scent of newly waxed floors and Windex glass cleaner. As

I became the subject of curious glances, a million questions went through my head. *Will my locker combination work? Who will sit by me at lunch? Will I have friends?*

The homecoming dance that year would be an important step in my social life. Loud music played, the deep bass echoing off the gymnasium's cinder block walls. The smell of newly waxed hardwood floors mixed with the stale scent of sweat that had compounded over years of basketball games. It was a predictable arrangement. The boys were backed up against the bleachers on one side. The girls alternated between the opposite bleachers and the dance floor.

Other than a select few males who could actually dance, most boys did not step onto the floor until the songs slowed down. Then there was a migration to the awkward embraces and rotational shuffling known as "the slow dance." During the first of such slow jams, a message was relayed to me from Donald Jenkens that Emily Malmberg wanted to dance with the new kid. Emily was tall, athletic, and popular. My fingertips tingled with the thought that I was liked. So I mustered up the gumption to ask her for the next dance.

The song was *Every Rose Has Its Thorn* by '80s glam metal band Poison. The song title should have been an omen that this would not be good, that I would be pricked and left bleeding. I navigated the dance floor over to the girls' side. I approached Emily. Her hair was perfect. Her smile was soft and warm. I attempted to speak over the blaring music:

"Do . . . do you want to dance?"

"What?" she said.

I increased my volume: "Do you want to dance?!"

"Uh . . . okay."

I remember that we stopped at the free-throw line of the basketball court. As an inexperienced slow dancer, I held her at a distance. We both stared over the other's shoulder, not wanting to make eye contact. I wanted to say something, but my mind was ticking like a metronome, trying to be keep the rhythm in my head: *one, two, three, four, one, two* . . . We shuffled in a circle, slowly rotating like a rotisserie chicken, and I soon felt like I was being roasted.

It wasn't until I returned to the boys' side that I was informed of Donald Jenkens's evil plan. He had *totally* lied about Emily wanting to dance with me, and she *totally* did *not* want to. Donald was bent over laughing in the corner with a posse of other "funny guys." Emily and a team of girls were huddled and giggling in the opposite corner. Under the dim lights of the gymnasium, I felt like a spotlight was on me. The music kept going, but the mood felt like silence. I stood on the sideline, alone.

I felt like a nobody. A joke. A worthless, skinny teenager that no one really cared about. I no longer belonged at my old school. And I certainly did not belong at my new one. *Do I belong anywhere? Does anyone really get me? Does anyone really love me?* Sunday School clichés and VBS Popsicle-stick crosses didn't seem to offer adequate spiritual answers anymore.

Jesus says, "Let the children come to Me; do not hinder them, for to such belongs the kingdom of God" (Mark 10:14). Why children? Because they are weak, vulnerable, and often shoved aside. Children are easily overlooked, abandoned, and abused. *But they belong to God, and the Kingdom belongs to them.* Children do nothing to belong. They belong simply because the Father makes them belong. It took a troubling high school experience to show me that belonging was based solely on the One I belong to.

You try so hard to belong. You try to make people love you, when you're already loved with a love that can't be earned. You belong to this God. You are loved by this Father. The blood-smeared cross of Jesus proves it. You were bought with a price. Your worth and your value are not based on your athletic ability, grade point average, or social network.

You belong to God and His kingdom precisely when you are embarrassed, ugly, guilty, abandoned, and alone. You have been initiated into a living community through trickling water and a powerful Word. So whether you feel like it or not, *you belong.*

I'm six feet three inches tall and skinny. I grew up in a remote northern town. I can't dance. I often instigate awkward moments. And I am completely comfortable with myself—because I belong to this God and this community called the Church.

Jeff Cloeter Jeff Cloeter is a pastor in St. Louis, Missouri. His Facebook profile lists the following: Favorite music: Johann Sebastian Bach, Pearl Jam, Jars of Clay, and Kings of Leon. Favorite movies: *Braveheart, Tommy Boy, Elf,* and *Finding Nemo.* Favorite books: *To Kill a Mockingbird,* and The Acts of the Apostles (in the Bible). Favorite quote: "I can raise and lower my cholesterol through pure concentration."—Dwight Schrutte from *The Office.* Pastor Jeff has a lovely wife, Bobbi, and two young children, Bella and Joshua.

. . . the holy Christian Church, the communion of saints . . .

The risen and ascended Christ forms the core of the Christian Church. Without the Spirit there is no true church.

> For where Christ is not preached, there is no Holy Spirit who creates, calls, and gathers the Christian Church, without which no one can come to Christ the Lord. (Large Catechism, Part II, paragraph 45)

Who and/or what does the Spirit use to call, gather, and enlighten today?

... the holy Christian Church, the communion of saints ...

So, until the Last Day, the Holy Spirit abides with the holy congregation or Christendom. Through this congregation He brings us to Christ and He teaches and preaches to us the Word. By the Word He works and promotes sanctification, causing this congregation daily to grow and to become strong in the faith and its fruit, which He produces. (Large Catechism, Part II, paragraph 53)

Who does the Spirit use in your church to teach the Word? How does the Spirit use this person?

...the holy Christian Church, the communion of saints ...

No strangers here . . .

> So then you are no longer strangers and aliens, but you are fellow citizens with the saints and members of the household of God, built on the foundation of the apostles and prophets, Christ Jesus Himself being the cornerstone, in whom the whole structure, being joined together, grows into a holy temple in the Lord. In Him you also are being built together into a dwelling place for God by the Spirit. (Ephesians 2:19–22)

Don't you just love going someplace and feeling right at home? Paul's words to the congregation of Ephesus remind us that there will be no strangers in heaven, but fellow citizens. What fellow citizen of heaven would you most like to get to know better? Why?

... the holy Christian Church,
the communion of saints ...

For by the grace given to me I say to everyone among you not to think of himself more highly than he ought to think, but to think with sober judgment, each according to the measure of faith that God has assigned. For as in one body we have many members, and the members do not all have the same function, so we, though many, are one body in Christ, and individually members one of another. Having gifts that differ according to the grace given to us, let us use them: if prophecy, in proportion to our faith; if service, in our serving; the one who teaches, in his teaching; the one who exhorts, in his exhortation; the one who contributes, in generosity; the one who leads, with zeal; the one who does acts of mercy, with cheerfulness. (Romans 12:3–8)

God gives His Church gifts and talents through the various members of the Body of Christ. What special gifts or talents has He given you? How could you use your gifts to serve the Church and others?

... the holy Christian Church, the communion of saints ...

D A Y • F I V E

> Jesus answered, "Truly, truly, I say to you, unless one is born of water and the Spirit, he cannot enter the kingdom of God. That which is born of the flesh is flesh, and that which is born of the Spirit is spirit. (John 3:5–6)

The bad news: heaven has an entry requirement, and you can't afford it.

The Good News: Jesus has already taken care of it.

In your journal today, write your own Good News/bad news faith statement.

Notes

Grace Boy
Bob Lenz

I've been speaking to young people for more than twenty years, and I finally wrote a book. I'm an author. Hold on! You don't know what kind of miracle that is. In fact, my daughter did a book report on my book

for school, and she actually has the same teacher that I had in high school. When he heard that the book report was about a book that I had written, he said with skepticism, "You're dad wrote a book? That's amazing!"

"Why?" my daughter responded.

"Because when he was in high school," he said, "I don't think he even *read* a book!"

I thought being an author would get me some recognition and compliments. Instead, I actually got some criticism and unexpected responses. You see, the content and title of my book is *Grace*. So instead of compliments, I got comments like, "Oh, you're one of *those* guys."

I responded with a puzzled look on my face: "*What* kind of guy?"

"You're one of those 'grace boys,'" they said. "You know, the kind of person who's light on sin and promotes easy faith. You don't use the Old Testament, and you've thrown out the Law."

I will not apologize for being a grace boy. (I think I'm in good company with someone else who said, "By grace alone.") But let me try to set the record straight. I believe in the Law. I believe that sin ruins our lives. I still believe the Bible to be true and that there's a real heaven and a real hell. But all my power to conquer sin hasn't been enough. No matter how hard I've tried, how much I hate sin, how much effort I give, I still don't measure up to the Law.

Not long ago, I took my family to Disney in Florida—is it Disney World or Disney Land? I can never remember. Well, whatever . . . Disneylandworld. My kids wanted to go on what they thought was the coolest ride: Space Mountain. So we got in line, which at Disney isn't so bad because they have videos and music along the way. But when we got in line, it was quite a distance from where the line was really supposed to start. Believe it or not, we got in line in the parking lot and waited with our five kids for an hour on the hot asphalt in 100-degree weather (that's *above* zero, by the way—you have to specify this kind of thing when you're from Wisconsin). Just standing there, I began sweating like crazy, so I asked my wife if it counted as exercise. After an hour, we finally got to the *beginning* of the line.

Then—there it stood. The dreaded measuring stick. (Some of you know where this is going.) With fear in my eyes, I watched as each of my kids stood next to it. Amber, check. Danielle, check. David, no problem. My redhead, Joyel, just made it. And then there was Tim, my youngest. As he stood next to the measuring stick, he tried to stretch and stand on his tiptoes. But it wasn't enough. He didn't measure up. He was a half inch too short.

Tim, with his dark black hair and big brown eyes, stood in fear. The attendant looked at him and said, "Sorry, son, you'll have to get out of the line." Tim turned and looked at me, and his lip began to quiver. A tear came down his face as he said, "Daddy, please?" I paused for a moment . . . then I punched the guy and we ran in. Wait. No. Obviously, I didn't do that.

See, the law was good. It was for Tim's safety. As hard as it was, I had to look at my son and say, "I'm sorry, Tim, you and your *mom* are gonna have to get out of line." Just kidding. But Tim didn't go on the ride.

The law, the measuring stick, was good. For Space Mountain, Tim was the only one who didn't measure up. But for the ride of real life, the Bible says that none of us measures up. Romans 3:10 says, "None is righteous, no, not one." Grace doesn't mean you throw out the Law. We have to look at what the purpose of the Law is. The Law comes to slay us, to bring us to the end of ourselves, to show us the way we're supposed to live, to reveal our sin, to show us our need for Christ. The Bible calls the Law our guardian to lead us to Christ (Galatians 3:24–25). We need to understand what the Law cannot do. The Law cannot make us righteous (which means being made right to enter into a relationship with Christ).

The Law is like a measuring scale. Standing on the scale doesn't help you lose weight, unless, of course, you stand there a long time without eating! I'm a bigger guy, so when I stand on the scale, it says, "Get off!" See, the scale doesn't help you lose weight. It tells you where you are. It shows you your need.

Grace doesn't okay sin. Grace doesn't lower the standard, the measuring stick. Actually, it makes the standard higher. There's only one way, one Mediator between God and man. There's only one ticket for this ride that's better than Space Mountain. This ride is called eternal life, and it's the greatest ride in the world—and even *out* of this world. So we need the Law and the Gospel. Law and grace. But make it clear: only in the death and resurrection of Jesus Christ, and by His free gift of grace to us, is eternal life found. And that's called grace. I guess I am a grace boy after all.

Bob Lenz Author and international speaker, Bob has an intense passion for sharing the love of Christ. Whether for an audience of 10 or 10,000, Bob connects with the hearts and minds of youth, helping them deal with real life while igniting their faith, instilling hope, and challenging them to make a difference in their world. Bob speaks to over 350,000 teens and parents across North America each year through school assembly programs and faith-based outreaches and events. In addition to speaking, Bob is founder and president of Life! Promotions, a nonprofit youth organization located in Appleton, Wisconsin, with a mission to instill hope in youth. Although speaking is a great privilege for Bob, his first commitment is to his family. His wife, Carol, and five children are a source of great joy and unending examples of committed love. Bob is on Facebook at http://www.facebook.com/boblenz.lifepromotions. and Twitter at: www.twitter.com/BobLenzLife. You can also visit his website at: www.lifespeaking.com.

. . . the forgiveness of sins . . .

In the Large Catechism, Martin Luther describes a vision of the Church and its role in the forgiveness of sins:

> Everything, therefore, in the Christian Church is ordered toward this goal: we shall daily receive in the Church nothing but the forgiveness of sin through the Word and signs, to comfort and encourage our consciences as long as we live here. So even though we have sins, the [grace of the] Holy Spirit does not allow them to harm us. (Large Catechism, Part II, paragraph 55)

As you journal today, consider how you might rewrite this message of comfort into your everyday language.

... the forgiveness of sins ...

D A Y • T W O

Yesterday you rewrote a statement about forgiveness and the Church. Today's quote is similar:

> For we are in the Christian Church, where there is nothing but [continuous, uninterrupted] forgiveness of sin. (Large Catechism, Part II, paragraph 55)

What does the concept of continuous, uninterrupted forgiveness mean for your daily life?

How does this affect how you deal with others?

... *the forgiveness of sins* ...

When it comes to sin we're all in the same place, and it isn't pretty.

> For there is no distinction: for all have sinned and fall short
> of the glory of God. (Romans 3:22–23)

But the rest of the message is the important part:

> ... and [all] are justified by His grace as a gift, through the
> redemption that is in Christ Jesus. (Romans 3:24)

How could you explain this Law-and-Gospel balance to someone who is new to the Christian faith?

... the forgiveness of sins ...

D A Y • F O U R

Therefore, if anyone is in Christ, he is a new creation. The old has passed away; behold, the new has come. All this is from God, who through Christ reconciled us to Himself and gave us the ministry of reconciliation; that is, in Christ God was reconciling the world to Himself, not counting their trespasses against them, and entrusting to us the message of reconciliation. Therefore, we are ambassadors for Christ, God making His appeal through us. We implore you on behalf of Christ, be reconciled to God. For our sake He made Him to be sin who knew no sin, so that in Him we might become the righteousness of God. (2 Corinthians 5:17–21)

What does it mean to be an ambassador for Christ?

Why does God entrust the message of salvation to sinners?

> My little children, I am writing these things to you so that you may not sin. But if anyone does sin, we have an advocate with the Father, Jesus Christ the righteous. He is the propitiation for our sins, and not for ours only but also for the sins of the whole world. (1 John 2:1–2)

John addresses these verses to "little children." He speaks these gentle words so that we can pass them along to future generations. How would you rewrite these words so that a young child could understand them?

Notes

Raising the Dead

Dion Garrett

I sat on the airplane with the tightness in my chest that you only feel in life's worst moments. I wasn't having a heart attack, thankfully, but my heart was breaking. Just hours before, my wife had appeared unexpectedly at the part-time job I was working to get through seminary to deliver the horrible news. My beloved grandfather had been killed that day in a car accident.

Most of the time, it's not supposed to be shocking when you lose a grandparent, but in my case, my Papa J. T. was in perfect health. Sharp minded and big hearted, he was the rock of our family. So as I sat there on that airplane with pain in my chest, a crazy thought came to mind. I remembered how Jesus had once raised His friend Lazarus from the grave— even after he had been dead for four days! So I started praying that God would raise my grandfather from the dead.

I know, it sounds absolutely insane! It kind of did to me that day too, but still, could it hurt to ask? And what if—*what if*—God wanted to raise up a dead man that day? Should I stand in His way?

I doubt that you will be surprised to hear that God didn't answer that prayer for my Papa J. T. *that day.* He was buried a few days later, and his body still lies there, waiting for Christ's return. But I want you to know that I have actually seen God raise a dead man to life, and it was only a dozen years earlier.

A claim like that demands some backstory, so here we go.

My relationship with God began at the baptismal font of a small country church when I was four years old. It was

Mother's Day, and I stood there next to my mom and my two sisters; we were all being baptized together. Conspicuously absent was my dad. He was there in the church that day, but he was not receiving the gift of Baptism with us.

My mom, my sisters, and I continued on in our faith for the years that followed, but my dad stayed away. We learned all about God, His instruction, His character and work. We learned how to pray and what the creeds said and meant. We learned about Jesus who reveals the full depths of the Father's love and who went beyond humanity's wildest imaginations in all He did to heal our broken relationship with God. I devoured it all. I paid close attention in Sunday School; I sang loudly the words of the hymns and the responses of the liturgies. It was all so real to me.

Then, as I started to grow up, God's realness began to fade for me. It's the same sort of feeling you have when you wake from a vivid dream. At first, it's so real that you're not sure that it didn't actually happen. Then, with time, you're sure it was all just a dream and that it didn't happen. After a long while, you barely even remember what the dream was about or why it affected you so. To me, God was beginning to become a blurry and ill-defined picture of goodness, morality, and fatherly care—but in all honesty, He was less than real.

Meanwhile, things at home were rough. My dad was a tortured man. One moment he was loving and involved, filled with life and joy about his family. The next moment he was angry, withdrawn. He was tormented by addictions too, ones that our whole family carried together in secret shame. We prayed for him. We loved him, but I hated his temper, his addictions, and his absence in church with us week after week.

Okay, enough of the background; you're ready to hear about the miracle I promised you.

It was February 1991. Things were bad that year. My younger sister was suffering from some depression problems; I think we all were. There was a man, a member at our church and a counselor, who reached out to help my parents deal with my sister. His interaction didn't seem to be very significant, so I was completely blindsided when I got home from school one day to find my dad already there. He sat us all down on the couch, which in my house was a sure sign that we were in trouble for something. I'll never forget what he said next: "Over the last few weeks, I've become convinced that God is real and Jesus is my Lord and Savior." He went on to say some other things, but I was reeling inside. Could this be true? Would it last? Even if it *did* last, what would it matter? What could it possibly change?

As it turns out, it changed everything. Over the next few weeks, I watched as God took my dad, who once was a dead man, and brought him to life.

That was a pivotal moment in my life. God, who had been growing fuzzy to me, came sharply into focus. He was *not* just some vague notion of goodness, morality, or fatherly love. He was *real* and *powerful*, and He had pursued my dad, tracked him down, won him over, brought a dead man to life, and changed a whole family's destiny forever. The constant refrain rolling around in my head became *People need to know that God is like this!*

There is a saying that I've fallen in love with. I can't trace its origin, but it's powerful all the same. Here it is: "Jesus Christ came *not* to make bad people good, but to make dead people live." I love that saying because it's true. God didn't send His Son into the world to fix our morality problems. No! Our problems go so much deeper. First and foremost, He came to take people who are nothing more than walking dead—dead in our sins, dead in our notions about what makes for a good life, dead in our hopes and dreams—and make them live!

That's exactly what Jesus says about Himself in John 5:24–25:

> "Truly, truly, I say to you, whoever hears My word and believes Him who sent Me has eternal life. He does not come into judgment, but has passed from death to life.

> "Truly, truly, I say to you, an hour is coming, and is now here, when the dead will hear the voice of the Son of God, and those who hear will live."

And so that's what I do now. I've committed my life to proclaiming the God I know—the God of Scripture, the God who brings dead people to life again. I hope you know Him that way too. He is so much more than a vague idea. He is real and powerful and personal and relentless in His pursuit of us. He can change family stories for generations. He can even raise the dead; in fact, He already has—His own Son first, but also all the rest of us who are in Christ. May you know Him and the life He came to bring you. There's nothing more important. May you also believe and go in His power to raise a world full of "walking dead."

Dion Garrett Pastor Dion Garrett is a recent transplant to the "holy city" of St. Louis, Missouri. Before that, he grew up and served near Detroit—Go Blue! (Note: that's "blue" as in University of Michigan, not "Blues" as in St. Louis hockey. His heart is forever devoted to the Red Wings.) His passion is for knowing God more and more and becoming more like His Son. He loves his wife, Jocelyn, and three great kids. He loves to sing loud (generally) and to worship, whether it's in church or in the car or in the shower ("You should hear me; it's definitely something!"). Dion is a Chipotle addict, a serious coffee drinker (quality, not quantity), and a health nut (which basically means that he eats *dark* chocolate instead of milk), but what he loves most is watching God's power unfold in people's lives. "Christ's working out His salvation in me, and it's incredible. I want the same gift for everyone," Dion says. "That's basically me. Maybe you're refreshed; maybe you think I sound a little wacky. Either way, it doesn't matter. A man much wiser and nobler than I'll ever be once said, 'Jesus must become greater, I must become less.' Sounds good to me." Dion is connected at Twitter username: diongarrett or Facebook: http://www.facebook.com/diongarrett. He also has his own website; www.diongarrett.com.

... the resurrection of the body ...

D A Y • O N E

> Then we will come forth gloriously and arise in a new, eternal life of entire and perfect holiness. For now we are only half pure and holy. So the Holy Spirit always has some reason to continue His work in us through the Word. He must daily administer forgiveness until we reach the life to come. At that time there will be no more forgiveness, but only perfectly pure and holy people. We will be full of godliness and righteousness, removed and free from sin, death, and all evil, in a new, immortal, and glorified body. (Large Catechism, Part II, paragraphs 57–58)

Luther describes our present condition in an interesting way: "half pure and holy." In your confirmation instruction, you may have learned this balance as "saint and sinner." What does living in the balance as saint and sinner mean for you?

What "sinner" things are particularly troublesome for you?

Luther also describes our "new, immortal, and glorified" bodies. What earthly body thing will you be happy to be rid of?

> For I know that my Redeemer lives,
>   and at the last He will stand upon the earth.
> And after my skin has been thus destroyed,
>   yet in my flesh I shall see God,
> whom I shall see for myself,
>   and my eyes shall behold, and not another. (Job
>   19:25–27)

In the midst of his suffering at the hands of Satan, Job gives this great witness of faith in the resurrection. How could you use these verses to refute those who saw the resurrection only as a spiritual state of existence?

... the resurrection of the body ...

> But we do not want you to be uninformed, brothers, about those who are asleep, that you may not grieve as others do who have no hope. For since we believe that Jesus died and rose again, even so, through Jesus, God will bring with Him those who have fallen asleep. For this we declare to you by a word from the Lord, that we who are alive, who are left until the coming of the Lord, will not precede those who have fallen asleep. For the Lord Himself will descend from heaven with a cry of command, with the voice of an archangel, and with the sound of the trumpet of God. And the dead in Christ will rise first. (1 Thessalonians 4:13–16)

Paul writes to the Church in Thessalonica concerning the second coming of Christ. Evidently some false teaching regarding the resurrection was spreading in the Church. How do Paul's words here make the truth very clear?

What could you tell someone who doubts the resurrection?

. . . the resurrection of the body . . .

>   And just as it is appointed for man to die once, and after that comes judgment, so Christ, having been offered once to bear the sins of many, will appear a second time, not to deal with sin but to save those who are eagerly waiting for Him. (Hebrews 9:27–28)

No second chances—how do these words from Hebrews refute the concept of reincarnation?

What's the truth concerning your status upon death?

What would you like others to say about you when you have died?

What's the most important thing they should know about you?

Notes

Birch Bark and Arrowheads

Bill Yonker

Some lessons are harsh. To be sure, if a lesson causes hardship or pain, it's probably a good lesson, but these can be harshest of all.

One summer helped me learn an important life lesson. I had finished the eighth grade and was gleefully anticipating my freshman year, but first there was a summer to enjoy. The highlight of the season was a trip to Grandpa Strege's in northern Wisconsin. Grandpa's house sat on a bluff at the edge of Tom Doyle Lake. A quick walk down the steps built into the hillside brought one right out to Grandpa's pier. Nestled up next to the pier was a holding pen for live, freshly caught sunfish and bluegill. On the other side, Grandpa kept his rowboat with a five-horsepower engine on the back of it.

We boys were allowed to use the boat to fish. My older brothers, Bob and Jon, could even go to the uninhabited island in the center of the lake, but that had been off-limits to me. I used to beg Grandpa to let me go to the island (legend had it there were tons of arrowheads to be found), but he said no. There was too much to hurt a lad of thirteen or fourteen who was by himself. Finally, though, I wore Grandpa down. On the last day of our stay, he said I could go to the island to search for arrowheads, but he would stay on the pier with his bullhorn, and if he called me, I had to come right home on the boat. I thought Grandpa had made a splendid deal, so I even shook hands on it.

You see, I had spent most of my time earlier in the summer making birch bark canoes while Bob and Jon were exploring the island. These toy canoes were fun to float, but that couldn't compare with the hope of finding real arrowheads left behind by ancient Native Americans. Bob and Jon liked my little birch bark boats, but I think they were secretly glad that there wasn't another person vying for the use of Grandpa's boat.

But now, on my last afternoon, Grandpa walked me down to the pier, watched me chug away in his little boat, and sat on the bench at the end of the pier with the bullhorn in his lap. The day was overcast, but there was plenty of light for me to be successful on my adventure and find arrowheads. Truly, I was thrilled as the boat ran aground on the sand at the island's edge. Pulling the boat well up onto the shore and tying it fast to a tree, I was ready to be the adventurer my soul longed to be.

I was immediately struck by all of the white birch trees that had been untouched. You see, birch bark tends to shred away from the trunk, so it is easy to strip off long, wide sheets of the stuff. Most of the birch trees on Grandpa's land had been shorn of their coating by yours truly. I couldn't pass up the bounty. I wanted to take some of this stuff back to Michigan to make canoes for my friends. I thought to spend only a few moments at this chore, but because of the abundance of bark and the ease of collecting it, I lost all track of time as I worked. That is, until I heard a clap of thunder and felt raindrops the size of nickels starting to fall.

Grandpa called for me across the lake on the bullhorn. He told me I had to come in "*now*." I turned in shock. My error in judgment was now all too clear to me. In acquiring birch bark,

I had traded away my opportunity to search for arrowheads. I was tempted to ignore Grandpa, but I knew a deal was a deal. I climbed back into the boat, preparing to beg Grandpa to let me go out again after the rain stopped.

By the time I made landfall, I was drenched, and so was my worried Grandpa. Lightning was streaking the skies, and a lake is no place for *anyone* to be during a storm, let alone Herb Strege's grandson. After securing the boat and hustling to the warmth of Grandpa's home with my sheets of birch bark, I started in with my litany of why Grandpa had to let me go out again after the rain stopped. Grandpa quieted my pestering with a "We'll see." But it became a moot point, for the rain didn't relent. I was heartsick as I went to bed. I prayed for an early sunrise, hoping I could go back to the island before we headed for home.

But the morning of the morrow brought more rain. Grandpa tried to reassure and comfort me by reminding me that the island would be there next summer. I could spend every day at the island if I wanted to then. That was my only consolation. I would make up for my mistake of gathering birch bark instead of hunting arrowheads during the next summer.

But it was not to be. That winter, Grandpa suffered his first heart attack. By spring, his home and his land had been sold, and he moved to Michigan with us for the last three years of his life. Never again did I stay at Grandpa's in Mc-Naughton, Wisconsin. Never again did I traverse the waters of Tom Doyle Lake or set foot on the island in the middle of it. Never again was I afforded the time or opportunity to look for arrowheads. Perhaps what is most ironic is that right at the northeast corner of my home on Tartans Drive in Dundee, Illinois, there stands a birch tree.

Now, I tell you that to tell you this: Why do we trade away our true hopes and dreams for things that really aren't that special? Why are we prone to gathering birch bark instead of searching for arrowheads? Haven't we all, at some time, been distracted from attending to the special things of life by focusing on the mundane and the routine? It's no wonder that we are painfully conscious that we have let our goals and hopes slip away because we were interrupted and distracted by the ordinary, the common, and the run-of-the-mill.

What has God set in your heart to achieve or accomplish? What plans or dreams of your youth have been set aside because you got sidetracked by the inconsequential and unimportant? Are we headed for the end of our lives with a sneaking suspicion that when we get there, we will realize we came by the wrong path?

Take time to slow down and consider these questions. It's not too late to start living—I mean really *living*—the rest of your life. But this cannot be done outside of seeking God's will first and foremost. Jeremiah reminds us of God's words: "'For I know the plans I have for you,' declares the Lord, 'plans to prosper you and not to harm you, plans to give you hope and a future'" (Jeremiah 29:11 NIV). God does have plans for you, and He has deposited them in you. No wonder Jesus says, "Seek first the kingdom of God and His righteousness, and all things will be added to you" (Matthew 6:33). When we seek God's kingdom first, we won't get sidetracked by the gathering of birch bark.

You know your future in heaven is secure. Jesus has bought and fully paid your entrance fee by His suffering and death. But how will you live until it's time for eternity? My encouragement is this: Don't waste your time gathering birch bark. Go search out the arrowheads of your dreams.

... and the life everlasting.

You see, all this is the Holy Spirit's office and work. He begins and daily increases holiness upon earth through these two things: the Christian Church and the forgiveness of sin. But in our death He will accomplish it altogether in an instant. (Large Catechism, Part II, paragraph 59)

At the death of a Christian, Christ's work is completed in an instant. The onetime sinner/saint becomes saint only. The sin-stained life is left behind forever. How can this message of joyful and completed transformation be a comfort to someone who has lost a Christian loved one?

... and the life everlasting.

In Handel's famous oratorio *The Messiah,* the baritone soloist sings these words from Paul's Letter to the Church at Corinth as a heralding trumpet accompanies him:

> Behold! I tell you a mystery. We shall not all sleep, but we shall all be changed, in a moment, in the twinkling of an eye, at the last trumpet. For the trumpet will sound, and the dead will be raised imperishable, and we shall be changed. For this perishable body must put on the imperishable, and this mortal body must put on immortality. (1 Corinthians 15:51–53)

Think about the music you listen to. What song would you use to announce the second coming of Jesus?

... and the life everlasting.

The apostle John describes eternal life in his Gospel:

> And this is eternal life, that they know You the only true
> God, and Jesus Christ whom You have sent. (John 17:3)

How would you describe eternal life to someone who has never heard about it?

... and the life everlasting.

Did you know that our heavenly Father planned your place in heaven before the world even began? Matthew 25:34 tells us:

> Then the King will say to those on His right, 'Come, you who are blessed by My Father, inherit the kingdom prepared for you from the foundation of the world.'

What does it mean to you that God provided for your salvation long before you were even born?

Write a prayer of thanksgiving in your journal today.

... and the life everlasting.

The Bible frequently uses the image of sheep and shepherd to describe our relationship with our heavenly Father:

> "My sheep hear My voice, and I know them, and they follow
> Me. I give them eternal life, and they will never perish, and no
> one will snatch them out of My hand." (John 10:27–28)

How is this description an accurate picture of your relationship with God?

In what other ways could you describe your relationship with your Savior?

Notes

Your Story
Gretchen Jameson

You have multiplied, O
LORD my God, Your wondrous
deeds and Your thoughts
toward us; none can compare
with You! I will proclaim and
tell of them, yet they are more
than can be told. (Psalm 40:5)

Now there are also many
other things that Jesus did.
Were every one of them to
be written, I suppose that the
world itself could not contain
the books that would be written. (John 21:25)

"That's a good one!"

"Did you hear about . . . ?"

"You're not going to believe this, but . . . ."

What makes a good story? The kind you can't get enough
of? The kind you just can't believe or wait to tell someone else
about? The kind that changes your life? We all want a story,
and to a greater or lesser degree, we might get that we all
have one. Sometimes, though, it takes a little digging to see
the blockbuster plot that is written into the story of our lives.

Trust me, it's there.

This book you're just about to finish is full of really great
stories. I hope that you've seen parts of your own life in the
lessons that they share. Maybe, though, you've been wonder-
ing, *What's my big story?*

When I was invited to write for this book, all sorts of ideas
ran through my head. I really wondered, *What is my story?
Do I even have one?* More problematic, when the stories were
happening around me, had I really seen them as interesting,
life-defining moments that were making me somebody new?

Probably not; and I struggled with how to recapture them here.

The thing about life is that it's filled with stories, and most of the time, you don't really recognize you're in the middle of living one until lots of time has passed, or somebody helps you connect the dots, or you have an opportunity—like this one for me—to dredge up some circumstance of your life and put it on paper. And in this case, try to make it meaningful.

In the end, it turned out that I couldn't pick just one story; and because I've never been really great at following the rules of the assignment, I decided not to share one. Instead, I'm going to tell you about my *non*story. I think this is a good idea because I have a suspicion that some of you reading this book wonder if your life is remotely story-worthy. Well, it is—and we'll get to that. But first, let's start my nonstory.

My teenage experience was pretty standard. I hated junior high because, like lots of people, I reached the incorrect conclusion that I was far more awkward, goofy, and just generally uncool than was actually the case. I guess you could say that I came into my own in senior high. The highlights: I worried about fitting in—and decided not to care. I played sports; actually liked homework; participated in student council and drama and choir. I had solid parents—pretty great parents, actually—and a quirky, fun younger sister. Our family ate dinner at the table almost every night, which I didn't realize was so unusual at the time. Looking back, it was a good experience. Adults would definitely see it that way—very well-rounded. It's just that in the moment, it didn't seem all that *defining*.

And of course, I knew Jesus. I had been raised in the Lutheran Church, and I attended worship every week. I taught a fourth-grade Sunday School class, and I led devotions for my sports teams. For a long time, I planned to grow up and be a lawyer. Somewhere along the line, though, some wires got crossed, and I ended up headed for a Lutheran college, where I studied to become a Lutheran high school teacher.

So what happened? What significant moment or story shaped my life and led me to make choices like these? Who influenced me? Where was I when I decided, *Aha! This is it! This is what my life and faith are going to be like*?

Here's the weird thing: I've gone on to live a life completely focused on serving the Church, first as a teacher and now as a public relations director, but I can't recall any "burning bush" moment that led me to it—you know, a moment when God sort of reached into the mix and made His calling in my life so incredibly obvious that I just couldn't miss it.

No. My nonstory is way more subtle. Here's how it played out:

Little by little, bit by bit, God consistently and fervently intersected my life with His Word. Sometimes His Word found me in the midst of formal worship as I grew up in the Church. And other times, He called to me through personal devotion and prayer time. Most of the time, His Word was carried to me by great coaches, teachers, my parents, and other caring adults—and yes, even by my friends. Gradually and over time, His Word shaped my life as I became a teacher and leader and spent time dwelling in Scripture so that I could do my work to the best of my ability. I suppose if it had all come at once, it would've made for a pretty epic moment, and I would be telling some seriously cool story here. Instead, God worked on my life in the details for a long, long time—and His work hasn't stopped.

The incredible thing about God's work in your life and in mine is that He knows precisely the kind of story each of us needs. Maybe for you He has planned a big moment that can't be denied. But maybe it won't be that clearly defined, and that can leave you frustrated if you worry too much about it.

At the end of his Gospel, John tells us that there is so much more to be said about the works Jesus did that there aren't enough books in the world to contain the story. As a former literature teacher, I am totally amazed by that statement! I would love to read those parts–the Miracle of the I-Don't-Know-What or the Feeding of the I-Can't-Guess-How-Many–that didn't make the first book, but happened nonetheless!

Then I start to think about what that statement really is saying: there were (and, let's say, *are*) so many other things that Jesus did that the world cannot contain the story. The story continues today. And it plays out in the moment-by-moment script God writes in your life as He works in you through Word and Sacrament. Jesus isn't finished.

The thing is, if you are worried that you don't have a story–or that somehow your faith journey is lacking because you can't put some incredibly significant moment into your faith timeline–that's perfectly all right. The real power in this book that you're reading is that it's not just Jeffrey's story, or Bob's story, or Paul's story–but that their stories are profoundly part of *His* story. And yours will be too. In fact, it already is.

In the end, our focus needs to be bigger than *What is my story?* If we operate with that kind of narrow perspective, our story will be all about the wrong things–us. And trust me: your story is so much better when it's taken from the Jesus Script.

When you look at Scripture, you see pretty quickly that most of the heroes of faith had these long, crazy, drawn-out stories. I often wonder if, in the moment, David and Moses and Rahab would have described their lives as incredible stories, or if they just figured that their lives were a great big mess. Taken alone, each of these stories is missing something; epic moments don't make epic stories. But put them together and connect them to the Savior of the world as the central character, and you've got one impressive, amazing, staggering, bigger-than-self, real-life tale.

Because Christ dwells in you, your story is a great chapter in the greatest story ever told. Your story and my story are completely connected to those in the Bible. I can say *I Believe* in the witness of all those other stories. And I can say *I Believe* in something bigger and better and way more interesting than my little nonstory. I believe in Jesus Christ, and His story is my story. What's yours?

Gretchen Jameson Gretchen likes to talk—a lot! She also likes to listen. In fact, she's made a career out of talking and listening, tweeting, e-mailing, Facebooking, making videos, podcasting, and using all sorts of media to talk about Jesus Christ. Gretchen graduated from Concordia University Nebraska (Bulldog pride!) and spent five years talking to students about history and directing theater arts at Milwaukee Lutheran High School and at Lutheran High School North in St. Louis. After lots of talking and listening with high school students, Gretchen spent the next six years talking as Associate Director of Communications for the Youth Ministry Office of The Lutheran Church—Missouri Synod. In 2008, she joined the team at Concordia Publishing House, where she talks about the CPH mission across the Church. Gretchen has a master's degree in public relations from Webster University in St. Louis, and she pretty much believes that talking, listening, and building relationships are the keys to achieving your goals, whether as an individual or for an organization. Gretchen and her husband, Leon (who also wrote for this book), live in Missouri. Together, they parent a carefree, energetic two-year-old, Sydney Grace. Gretchen enjoys cooking gourmet meals, all kinds of exercise, traveling to everyday and exotic locations, and spending time with youth. You can talk with Gretchen online at Twitter.com/gmjameson.

Amen.

For here in all three articles God has revealed Himself and opened the deepest abyss of His fatherly heart and His pure, inexpressible love. He has created us for this very reason, that He might redeem and sanctify us. (Large Catechism, Part II, paragraph 64)

In the last section you learned that God planned for your salvation before the beginning of the world. Here we learn we were created so that God could redeem and sanctify us. How was Jesus part of the plan from the beginning?

Amen.

Did you know you were adopted? No, really! In this Letter to the Church at Ephesus, Paul tells the people:

> Blessed be the God and Father of our Lord Jesus Christ, who has blessed us in Christ with every spiritual blessing in the heavenly places, even as He chose us in Him before the foundation of the world, that we should be holy and blameless before Him. In love He predestined us for adoption as sons through Jesus Christ, according to the purpose of His will, to the praise of His glorious grace, with which He has blessed us in the Beloved. (Ephesians 1:3–6)

Why is your adoption important? How can you thank God for your adoption as His son or daughter?

Amen.

John concludes his revelation with these dramatic words:

> He who testifies to these things says, "Surely I am coming soon." Amen. Come, Lord Jesus! The grace of the Lord Jesus be with all. Amen. (Revelation 22:20–21)

We conclude the Apostles' Creed with the word "Amen" as well. *Amen* literally means "So be it." Why do you suppose both Revelation and the Creed end with this same word?

How is it an appropriate word to end all of your prayers?

Amen.

For the Son of God, Jesus Christ, whom we proclaimed among you, Silvanus and Timothy and I, was not Yes and No, but in Him it is always Yes. For all the promises of God find their Yes in Him. That is why it is through Him that we utter our Amen to God for His glory. (2 Corinthians 1:19–20)

Yes! In what ways is Jesus Christ your "yes"?

Amen.

D   A   Y   •   F   I   V   E

As each has received a gift, use it to serve one another, as good stewards of God's varied grace: whoever speaks, as one who speaks oracles of God; whoever serves, as one who serves by the strength that God supplies—in order that in everything God may be glorified through Jesus Christ. To Him belong glory and dominion forever and ever. Amen. (1 Peter 4:10-11)

You've reached the end. Now what? How will you use the information you've read and written in your journal?

Notes